Paul of Tarsus

What made the greatest enemy of the
followers of Jesus willingly accept hatred, imprisonment and the constant threat of death
for the cause he was once determined to
destroy?

GARY

This is the dramatic re-creation of the life of
Paul, the man who threatened to wipe out the
Christian church but who, after the moment
that changed his life, travelled hundreds of
miles to spread the message he had called
blasphemy. It captures the excitement and
uncertainty of those days, the spirit of the
world in which Paul lived and the dynamism
of his personality. It brings alive
his times of loneliness and disappointment
as well as his triumphs. Most of all it gives an
understanding of the power which completely
changed Paul and his friends, and caused
them to start the revolution which still
continues.

An Aslan Lion Book

PAUL
OF TARSUS

Joy Harington

LION PUBLISHING

LION PUBLISHING
Icknield Way, Tring, Herts

First edition 1961 Brockhampton Press
Revised and reprinted in this
Aslan paperback edition
by Lion Publishing 1978

ISBN 0 85648 125 4

Text set in 10/12 pt Photon Baskerville, printed by
photolithography, and bound at The Pitman Press, Bath

cover photograph courtesy of Alan Hutchinson Library.

Contents

1
The Feast
of Pentecost

IT was the Feast of Pentecost. The day when all over the world Jews remember the time when God gave the Law to Moses on Mount Sinai.

For a week they had been pouring into Jerusalem. From the east and the west they came, rich and poor, light skinned, dark skinned, scholars, merchants, doctors, lawyers, tradesmen, farmers. Jews from the mountains of Cilicia in their cloaks of goats' hair, Jews from Africa burnt as black as ebony, Jews from Macedonia who had forgotten their mother tongue and spoke only Greek, Jews from Rome who wore the toga.

They filled the city streets and thronged the temple courts, and from the villages of Galilee and Judea peasant farmers and their families marched along the dusty roads, their camels and donkeys laden with the first fruits of the harvest which they brought to offer to God in the temple on the great day of the Feast of Pentecost.

Not many people in those busy streets remembered a man called Jesus of Nazareth who had been crucified outside the city seven weeks ago.

It was early morning on the day of the great feast when John Mark, a boy of sixteen, crossed the courtyard to his mother's house. On his shoulder he carried a pitcher of water he had fetched from the well at the end of the street. A cock crowed, but otherwise the early morning streets were silent. Mark was surprised to find that a dozen or so people had gathered in the courtyard and were waiting silently and, it seemed, expectantly. Some of them were staring up at the window of the upper room, the room used by his mother's guests, the men from Galilee.

Mark crossed the courtyard and climbed the outside stairway. As he opened the door of the upstairs room, his mother who stood just by the door turned and put her finger to her lips. Mark glanced round the room. They were all there, all except Judas, of course. His place had been taken by a man Mark didn't know very well, a man named Matthias. Simon Peter sat between James and John Zebedee. These were the three that had been the master's closest friends. Mark recognized the silence that seemed to throb in the upper room. It meant that the twelve were praying. Very quietly he put down his pitcher, poured a little water over his dusty feet and then took his place beside his mother. After a little while Peter spoke. He spoke to someone else who was in that upstairs room with them. Someone Mark knew was there, but whom he could not see.

'Lord Jesus, when you lived among us you opened our minds so that we understood the scriptures. We ask you to be with us on this holy day of Pentecost.'

Mark and his mother joined with the men as one by one they joined in the prayer.

'Be with us on this holy day of Pentecost.' There was a pause, then Peter spoke again:

'Send us the power you promised, Lord, that we may be able to spread the good news of God's kingdom to all his people gathered in Jerusalem.'

This time everyone prayed aloud, 'Send us the power, Lord.'

Silence filled the little room again. Mark was aware of a

strange, almost unbearable excitement tingling through his body. What was it like? When had he known it before? Then he remembered. When he was a little boy he had stayed with his Uncle Barnabas in Cyprus when there had been an earthquake. He remembered the strange, breathless, expectant silence that enveloped the island beforehand. That was how it was now. Something—something was about to happen that would shake the world. Mark was trembling, he bit his lips hard to stop the shout—was it of joy or of terror?—that wanted to burst out of his throat.

His eyes searched the faces of the others. His mother's eyes were shut, but he knew her heart was beating rapidly; John's face had a look Mark had never seen before, as though the flesh was transparent and a light burned behind it. Peter sat so still, he might have been carved out of rock. And Mark felt in his own face and body the burning light; the rock-like stillness; the beating heart; the stirring of life itself. The faces swam before his eyes, merging into one face. The bodies into one body. One body waiting—waiting—waiting. Mark was the first to hear it, a sound, distant at first, but growing in volume like the sound of a rushing wind. Nearer and nearer it came until the room and the waiting body was filled with it. The light that Mark had seen and felt behind the face suddenly burst through like flames.

The stillness was broken as one after another the waiting men leapt to their feet—and a great shout went up.

'The Lord has sent his Holy Spirit to us.'

In the courtyard below the waiting people were surprised to hear shouts, laughter, and snatches of psalms burst from that upstairs room that had been so quiet.

'What's happened, are they drunk or what?' the people asked each other.

Down the stairs poured the disciples still singing and shouting.

'These men are out of their minds,' said the people, but they followed them as they marched along the narrow streets towards the temple.

In the temple courtyard, the Rabbi Gamaliel sat with his circle of pupils. He was reading to them from the scroll of the prophet Jeremiah:

'The Lord says, "The time is coming when I will make a new covenant with the people of Israel ..."' Suddenly the rabbi's voice was drowned by a great noise of shouting and singing from outside the temple gates. People began to run across the courtyard to see what was happening. Gamaliel dismissed his class and the students joined the crowds at the Beautiful Gate.

The singing and shouting came closer and closer as a party of twelve men climbed the narrow street leading up to the temple.

'Who are they?' asked a tall stranger from Cyprus.

'It's the Galileans,' he was told.

'Galileans?'

'Yes. I thought they'd left the city by now.'

'Who are they?' asked a young man from Tarsus, one of Gamaliel's pupils.

'Some new sect. Followers of a Nazarene called Jesus.'

'Is he with them?'

'Jesus? No. He's dead and buried. Crucified last Passover.'

A shout rang out above the other voices.

'Jesus lives!'

The twelve had now reached Solomon's Porch and the people were crowding round them.

The man from Cyprus turned to his friend. 'Come on, Saul, let's hear what these Galileans are shouting about.'

He strode over to the porch. Saul followed.

The joy and excitement of the Galileans had infected the holiday crowds who called out to them good-naturedly, 'Shame on you. Drunk so early in the morning!'

Simon Peter raised his arms and the crowd grew quiet. His voice was charged with excitement. 'Men of Judea and all you here in this holy city, listen to what I have to say. We are not *drunk* as you might imagine ... why it's only nine in the morning!'

A ripple of laughter ran through the crowd and a voice shouted, 'What's got into you then?'

'The Holy Spirit.'

'*What?*'

'What do you mean, "Holy Spirit"?'

Again Peter raised his arms. 'Listen then, and I'll tell you. Today a great prophecy has come true and you, you are the witnesses.'

The crowd were quiet now, expectant. Peter looked round the circle of faces. 'I'm no scholar like some of you gentlemen,' he said, 'but I remember learning these words when I was a boy. "I will pour out my Spirit on everyone: your old men will have dreams and your young men will see visions. At that time I will pour out my Spirit even on servants, both men and women." This is the prophecy that you see fulfilled. God's own Spirit poured out on everyone, on me and these men here who have seen things more wonderful than visions and dreams. . . . We have seen cripples walk, the blind see, the sinner become a saint—the dead live again.' A murmur of disbelief ran through the crowd. Peter raised his voice. 'Yes, we have seen all these things, and not only us, many among you have seen them—does nobody here remember Jesus the Nazarene?'

Only one man did. 'Do you mean the man who was crucified last Passover?'

'Yes. The man who was sent to you by God and whom you crucified.'

Voices broke out in the crowd. 'It wasn't us put him to death, it was the Romans.'

'It was one of his own friends. One of you lot who betrayed him.'

But Peter was not to be shaken. 'He was sent by God to you, he was betrayed by man to you. And you handed him over to those ungodly men who nailed him to a cross and murdered him. . . But death could not hold him. Neither our blindness, our wickedness, nor our fear could defeat God's plan. Do you remember these words, "You will not abandon me in the world of the dead; you will not allow your faithful servant to rot in the grave"?'

Some of the listeners were getting impatient and one called

out, 'What has this to do with Jesus the Nazarene? You're quoting from the holy psalmist David.'

'Brother,' said Peter, addressing himself directly to the speaker, 'one thing at least you will agree. David died and was buried and his tomb is with us to this day. So it is obvious, isn't it, that David was speaking, not of himself, but of someone who would come after him? Of the Messiah. And again, when David said, "The Lord said unto my Lord 'Sit at my right hand' " his vision was of the Messiah, the Christ, sitting at the right hand of God. A Messiah who was to be one of his descendants, who would live as a man among men, who would throw off the shackles of death and then to return to God the Father who would send his Spirit, the Spirit of the living Christ, to live within men... This is exactly what has happened. Jesus of Nazareth was a descendant of David. He lived with us preaching about the kingdom of God, and we saw the signs and wonders that God performed through him. But, here is the absolute proof. Although he was betrayed and sentenced to death and crucified; although he was taken down from the cross and buried in a tomb—God brought him back life again. All of us here have seen him, time after time since the Passover we have talked with him, touched him, eaten with him. And last week we were talking to him as I'm talking to you now, over there on the Mount of Olives, when all of a sudden it was as though a cloud enveloped him and took him from our sight. We knew then what had happened. He had gone back into heaven to sit on the right hand of God the Father. And from our Father he has claimed for us the long-promised gift of the Holy Spirit.' Peter's voice rose again to a shout. 'It is yours, yours to claim now if you will ask forgiveness for your sins and be baptized in the name of Jesus the Christ.'

There was no doubt that Peter's astonishing words had gripped his audience. A wave of excitement ran through the crowd as the question, 'Jesus, the Christ?' was picked up and tossed from one to another. Only Saul, the young man from Tarsus, stood silent and horrified.

At last a single word broke from his lips. 'Blasphemer!'

The Cypriot turned, startled by his friend's outburst. 'What if it's the truth, Saul?'

'Barnabas!' It was like a cry for help.

The crowd had now worked themselves up to a pitch of feverish excitement. Peter's voice rang out above the rest. 'Come on then, as many of you as will. Come back with us to our lodgings to eat and drink and be baptized.'

The noise gradually died away as the crowd followed the Galileans down the street. Barnabas would have gone with them. He spoke again to his friend. 'They're staying at my sister's house. This one they call the Messiah stayed there too right up to the time of his arrest.'

'You mean you know them?'

'No, not yet. I've only been over from Cyprus two days. But my young nephew wrote me about the men from Galilee and of the one who had been crucified. It seemed like a nasty dangerous business to me, and I didn't like my sister to be mixed up in it. But now. . .'

'They've fooled you with their lies!'

'It isn't so much what they said, it's the joy and the life that's in them. I mean—well, here are a bunch of men miles away from home, their leader executed as a criminal. You'd expect them to be defeated—afraid—revengeful—wouldn't you?'

Saul's voice was harsh. 'Have you gone mad, Barnabas? Don't you see that his monstrous deceit is just the way for these defeated fanatics to revenge the death of their leader?' Now the words poured out. 'A criminal is executed. His friends steal the body, and then after working on the people's feelings by quotations they have cunningly sifted from the scriptures, they announce that their leader has come to life again. Nobody but them has seen him, you notice. And in case you should ask, "Where is he now?" they tell you he has ascended into heaven, "In a cloud" if you please. . . Why, one could laugh if it weren't for the damnable and wicked blasphemy.'

'But what would be the point of it? What would they possibly hope to gain?'

'Whatever it was their leader was out to gain. He wasn't

crucified for nothing, you may be sure. Keep away from them, Barnabas, for the love of God.'

But Barnabas was unmoved by his friend's words. He strode off down the street leaving Saul standing alone.

Mary was busy. Busier than she had been for years. The court-yard below her window was crowded, and excited voices floated up to her as she bustled about preparing plate after plate of food. She handed a laden tray to the little servant-girl.

'There, Rhoda, take that lot down, and come and tell me if they need more.'

As Rhoda moved to the door Mark burst in with a shout, 'Look who's here, mother.'

Mary held out her arms to the tall young man who stood smiling in the doorway. 'Barnabas! How wonderful! I knew you'd try and get here for the feast.'

Her brother came swiftly to her and embraced her affectionately.

'Mark, bring some wine for your uncle and then go to the well for more water.'

When Mark had gone out with the empty pitcher, Barnabas said, 'Mary, I've just heard one of your Galileans preaching in the temple.'

Mary beamed. 'You were there, were you? That was Simon Peter. They say he spoke like one of the old-time prophets, as if he was inspired. Thousands followed him here.'

Barnabas spoke with a sudden urgency. 'Mary, do you believe that this Jesus rose from the dead?'

Mary looked at her brother. 'He told them that, did he?'

'Yes he did.' His voice was sharp. Mary quietly went on cutting the bread.

'Mary, why did he tell them that?'

'Because it's true.'

'Then, *you* believe he was the Messiah?'

'I know it.'

His sister's simple acceptance of something so amazing, so tremendous, made her a stranger to him. For a moment he felt cold and shut out. His voice was a little shaky when he spoke. 'But . . . what does it mean?'

Mary looked at her brother sympathetically. 'Peter's always telling us not to try and see too far ahead. "Give us this day our daily bread." That's a prayer the master taught them. None of us knows what the end will be, he says. All we can do is try to follow in the master's footsteps.'

'But what about those who never knew him?'

Mary's calm voice now held a touch of excitement. 'But you can know him. That's the whole point. You've only got to believe. Oh, I'm no preacher, I can't find the words, I only know that it's like a door opening, like being born into a new life.'

Barnabas turned away from her and looked down from the window on to the excited crowds in the courtyard below. From the hubbub of voices one rose above the others.

'Jesus is Lord.'

'Some would call it blasphemy,' he said.

In the temple courtyard Gamaliel sat with his circle of pupils. The young man Saul stood facing him.

'Master, would you tell us your opinion of the sect known as "The Nazarenes"?'

'Nazarenes?'

Saul could not keep the revulsion from his voice. 'The men from Galilee who followed Jesus of Nazareth.'

'Oh, those!' Gamaliel spoke as usual with thoughtful liberality. 'They've quite a following, haven't they? Well, from all I hear they have been doing a great deal of good in the city. Feeding the poor, caring for the widows and fatherless, and teaching the people to lead godly lives.'

Saul's voice cut across his master's like a whip. 'Master, with respect, I think you cannot know the things they are teaching. With my own ears I have heard them speak blasphemy.'

'Blasphemy? That is a serious charge. Take care what you say, my son.'

'Master, I only report what I have seen and heard. Last week a Galilean fisherman who seems to be their spokesman publicly declared that Jesus the Nazarene who was justly crucified was Israel's Messiah.'

'Well?'

Saul curbed his anger with difficulty and his voice rose. 'They teach that this . . . this hanged criminal rose from the dead and now sits at the right hand of God. Is that not blasphemy?'

The Rabbi Gamaliel looked at his pupil, Saul. He loved this young man, one of the most earnest and deeply religious of his class, but he recognized the dangerous light of fanaticism in the dark angry eyes. He spoke to him quietly, but with firm authority. 'God has not made us to be judges of each other, Saul. He expects us to be vigilant, not bigoted. We do not know in what age or in what manner he will send his Messiah to his people, but we have been warned by the prophets that there will be signs and wonders that men will not believe though they see them. I think men have come to look for the sort of Messiah they have created out of their imagination. God's ways are not our ways, Saul, and time will show whether the teaching of the Nazarenes is true or false.'

Across the courtyard the sweet notes of the silver trumpets rang out, summoning people to the afternoon service. Gamaliel rose and dismissed his pupils. Saul stood alone, trembling with anger and bitter disappointment.

Among the people pouring through the Beautiful Gate for the afternoon service was a man carried on a friend's back. His face and shoulders were those of a man in the prime of life, but his thin lifeless legs might have belonged to a boy of ten. His friend propped him up against one of the great pillars.

The cripple spoke cheerfully, as one who was used to this routine. 'You'll come back for me after the service?'

'That's right. Good luck.'

And he joined the crowds in the temple courtyard.

Immediately the man began his sing-song cry. 'Have pity on one crippled from birth.'

Two men, fishermen from Galilee, were entering the gate. As they passed him the beggar stretched out his hand. 'Help, good sirs, help for a cripple.'

Peter and John stopped and looked at each other. The same memory had flashed into each mind. A memory of their master passing through just such a crowd and a lame man crying out for help. The beggar had turned his head away and was appealing to others. 'Have pity on one crippled from birth.'

Peter's voice rang out, 'Look at us.'

Eagerly the man turned to look at them, stretching out his hand again. Looking directly into his eyes Peter spoke now with a quiet intensity. 'I have no silver or gold, but I will give you what I do have . . . In the name of Jesus Christ of Nazareth . . . get up and walk!'

The man stared at them in astonishment. Peter seized the outstretched hand and pulled him to his feet, John supporting him on the other side. The look of astonishment on the man's face changed to incredulous wonder. Peter and John felt his strong arms trembling as the man leant heavily on their shoulders. At first he spoke in a whisper. 'I'm standing . . . my feet, my ankles. I can feel them . . . they're tingling, they're hurting. . . they're coming to life!' And then, a shout—'Praise be to God . . . Praise the Lord . . . I can stand.'

'Now walk.'

'*Walk?*'

'Walk into the temple and give thanks to God.'

Leaning on Peter and John the man managed a first hesitant step, then another, then another. At each step he gained strength and by the time they joined the crowds in the temple courtyard he was actually skipping and leaping.

From inside the temple came the voices of the men and boys of the Levite choir. In the thronged courtyard all was quiet as the worshippers listened.

Suddenly the silence was shattered and all eyes turned towards the Beautiful Gate as hoarse excited shouts mingled with the voices of the choir.

'The Lord God has given life to my legs. Thanks be to God who has seen the suffering of his servant and had pity on me!'

The devout worshippers began to murmur, first with

irritation, then with interest.

'It's the beggar from the Beautiful Gate. He's walking.'

'But he's been crippled all his life. I remember him being carried to the gate when he was a child.'

'Look at those two with him, aren't they two of the Nazarenes?'

The singing from the temple had come to an end, and the voices in the courtyard rose in excitement as the news of the crippled beggar spread.

'It's a miracle.'

'The lame beggar's been healed.'

'It's the Nazarenes.'

The young man Saul was instantly alert, and as the crowds surged towards Solomon's Porch where Peter and John had led the beggar, he stood alone once more.

He was not alone for long. Down the temple steps came the high priest, Annas, accompanied by the commander of the temple. As Saul saw them conversing together, he made up his mind to speak. As a Pharisee he was bitterly opposed to the priestly régime, but finding no support from his rabbi he swallowed his pride and decided to appeal to the most powerful Jew in Jerusalem. He approached the high priest. 'My Lord.' Annas turned. 'The Nazarenes are preaching at Solomon's Porch again.'

'How many?'

'Only two today, my lord, but they've gathered an enormous crowd. A crippled beggar claims to have been healed by them.'

'It is not a sin to heal the sick.'

But the commander immediately sensed danger. 'That's true, my lord, but you remember the disturbance that the so-called miracles of their leader caused.'

Annas did remember. 'Jesus the Nazarene? But he was a blasphemer.'

Saul spoke urgently. 'These men, too, speak blasphemy, my lord. They say that this Jesus is the Messiah and that God has raised him from the dead.'

The high priest turned to his commander and spoke sharply.

'That must be stopped.'

'Yes, my lord. Shall I arrest them?'

Annas nodded. 'But as on that other occasion, take them quietly.'

The commander nodded, and summoning two of his guards moved off in the direction of Solomon's Porch. The high priest went on his way. Saul stood watching, a flicker of triumph on his face.

In the upstairs room Mary and Mark were arranging their mattresses for the night. The house was so crowded since the twelve Nazarenes had been staying with them that Mary and her son had to sleep in this room.

'Have you locked up, Mark?'

'Not yet. Peter and John aren't in yet.'

'Are you sure?'

'Yes. The others are all here, but not those two.'

'Where can they have got to?'

There was the sound of feet hurriedly mounting the stairs.

'This'll be them.'

Mark went to the door and looked down the stairs. 'No. It's Uncle Barnabas.'

Barnabas burst in. He seemed strangely elated.

'Sorry to come so late, Mary, but I've just decided something, and I had to come and tell you.'

'Whatever is it, brother?'

'I'm not going back to Cyprus.'

'But the estate?'

'I'm going to sell it.'

'What are you going to do then? Set up business in Jerusalem?'

'I want to stay here with you and Mark. May I?'

'Of course, brother. But what will you do?'

Barnabas came over to her and took her hands. 'I want to join these Nazarenes and work with them.'

'Barnabas!'

'Listen, Mary, when I've sold my land in Cyprus and got the

money, I want to give it to them.'

'All of it?'

'Yes, all of it. It's never brought me any happiness. Just a lot of work and worry, and, worse than that, it was becoming a sort of master over me. A master I had to serve. Well, that's the wrong way round, isn't it? Money should be a servant not a master, and it seems to me I've found the place where it can serve best.'

Mary didn't speak.

'Don't you think that's right, Mary?'

'I know it's right.' She kissed her brother warmly.

Mark was equally excited by the news. 'I wish Peter was here so we could tell him.'

'Where is he?'

'We don't know,' said Mary. 'He went down to the temple this afternoon with John and hasn't been home since, not either of them, not even for their supper. They're usually all in before this. We'll have to leave the door on the latch, Mark, we can't stay up all night.'

In a prison cell in the temple precincts Peter stood looking out of the small grille window. It was early morning and a cock crowed. The sound filled Peter with a fearful memory. John heard him whisper:

'Oh, master, stay near me.'

John came to him. 'He told us it would be like this, Peter. Do you remember? That we would be persecuted for his sake.'

'Yes.' The cock crowed again and this time Peter's voice drowned the noise. 'I'll not deny him this time.'

The council was assembled. The court sat in a semi-circle, the high priest and Sadducees on one side, the Pharisees on the other. Their pupils, including Saul, occupied the front three rows. Gamaliel was addressing the attentive assembly.

'I would like to remind the court that these Nazarenes have, so far, done nothing that is against the law of the Pharisees. The doctrine of the resurrection that they preach is, as my lord knows, one of our strongest beliefs.'

The high priest was impatient. The strict rules of the Pharisees did not interest him.

'Yes, yes. We know. The court has not met to argue on that point.'

Gamaliel was not to be put off.

'Has it then met, my lord, because of the so-called cure of a beggar?'

Annas motioned to one of the elders who rose to his feet and with bored deliberation delivered a formal reply to the old rabbi.

'If a charge is brought against these men it will not be that they preach the doctrine of the resurrection, nor that a cripple is said to have been cured by them, but that these men are preaching that the *Nazarene Jesus* has risen from the dead, and that in *his name* they can heal the sick.' He sat. The high priest spoke.

'Are you satisfied, Rabbi Gamaliel?'

'For the moment, yes, my lord.'

Gamaliel sat down in his place and Annas called to one of the guards.

'Bring the prisoners in.'

The guard went out. Annas relaxed and spoke to the council.

'I don't think the court will be here for very long. If I remember rightly these Nazarenes are ignorant, cowardly men. Brave enough when surrounded by an admiring crowd, but in the face of authority they run. All of them deserted their leader when he was arrested.'

The guard opened the door of the cell.

'The high priest's waiting for you.'

As Peter followed John to the door, the cock crowed for the third time.

They left the cell followed by the guard.

In the council chamber the third prisoner faced the court. He stood proudly, if a little awkwardly on his thin, strong legs, his jaw had dropped at the sight of the formidable assembly, but when the guard entered with Peter and John a delighted grin lit his face and he shuffled along to stand as close beside them as he could. The elder, who was acting as the prosecuting counsel, rose.

'Simon Bar Jonah, John Bar Zebedee and Jacob Bar Ezra. The council would have you understand that you are not here under a charge, but in order that inquiries may be made about a certain incident that took place at the Beautiful Gate yesterday afternoon ... Jacob Bar Ezra?'

'Yes?' The beggar was quite cheerful now.

'How old are you?'

'I don't know exactly. But over forty, that I do know.'

'What is your trade?'

'Well, I've never had a trade, sir.'

'Why is that?'

'Because I was a cripple, sir. Couldn't walk or stand.'

'A cripple? For how long?'

'Ever since I was born, sir.'

One of the Pharisees rose to interject:

'There are witnesses to testify to the truth of that, my lord.'

The elder ignored the interruption and continued his questioning.

'Will you tell the court how it is that you are able to stand and walk now?'

'I'd be glad to, sir.' The beggar turned joyfully to face the court. 'It was like this: I was sitting at the Beautiful Gate yesterday afternoon, that's where I've always sat because the most people come in that way to the temple in the afternoon ...'

The elder interrupted this reminiscent flow. 'Just tell the court what happened.'

Totally unrepentant, the man continued: 'Well, along came these two, and I held out my hand for money like I always do. They stopped and this one, Peter they call him, said, "Look at us". So I did, and then he took hold of my hand, and all at once I felt the strength begin to flow into my legs right down to my ankle bones. I've never been able to feel anything in them before. Just dead they were. Then he said, "Stand up and walk", and I stood! Not only stood, I walked and ran and jumped—like this.' And in front of that solemn gathering the beggar, his arms round the shoulders of his friends, kicked his legs in the air, jumped up and down, and ran shakily to the door and back. There was a murmur of laughter from the young students, but the elder's voice was stern.

'That is enough.' He turned to Peter. 'Simon Bar Jonah, you have heard this man's evidence. Is what he says true?'

'Yes.'

Almost persuasively the elder continued:

'Will you tell the court by what power or in whose name you were able to perform this cure?'

There was only a second's pause before Peter's voice rang out.

'In the name of Jesus Christ of Nazareth whom you crucified and whom God raised from the dead.'

There was no laughter now. Only a few shocked whispers.

The elder turned to John.

'What do you say, John Bar Zebedee?'

John's young voice was charged with joy. 'The man was healed by the power of Jesus the Christ.'

In the dead silence that followed, Saul noticed a flicker of uneasiness on the high priest's face. Then he snapped an order to the guard.

'Take the prisoners to wait outside.'

The three men were hustled out. Again Annas broke the silence.

'The danger is greater than we imagined. These men have become bold. It's quite clear that in a spirit of revenge for their leader's death, they are trying to work upon the people's feelings and incite them against their rulers. If we let them go they'll cause as much trouble as the Nazarene did.'

The elder who had listened to the evidence reminded Annas of the most immediate danger.

'There's no doubt, my lord, that a miraculous healing has taken place.'

The high priest continued to think aloud:

'And the people know it. If we keep these men in prison they will be regarded as martyrs and the situation will be worse than it is now. It might even provoke the Roman authorities.'

Gamaliel rose to his feet.

'May I suggest, my lord, that there is no real harm in these men. Both are God-fearing Jews. It is only their exaggerated ideas about their leader that could be dangerous. Could my lord not explain to them that, since all power comes from God, it is wrong to use the name of their dead leader.'

Annas was grateful for any way out of the dilemma.

'I accept your suggestion, Rabbi Gamaliel ... Recall the prisoners.'

A guard opened the door and beckoned. Peter, John and the beggar came in and stood, as before, in front of the court.

The high priest's voice was ingratiating as he addressed the two Nazarenes.

'In view of the undoubted benefit that you have somehow brought to this man, the court has decided to overlook certain aspects of your case and set you free to continue your good works, on one condition. On no account are you to preach or to heal in the name of Jesus of Nazareth.'

There was a moment's pause. Then Peter spoke.

'My lord high priest, you must judge whether it is right in the sight of God for us to obey him or obey you.'

Annas seemed embarrassed, but his tone changed to one of bullying.

'I warn you, if you speak the name once more, the punishment will be severe.'

John did not hesitate for a moment.

'We speak of the things we have seen and heard, my lord, we cannot stop.'

'You have heard my command.'

But Peter had the last word.

'We must do as God commands, my lord, for it is not proper to put the commands of men above those of God.'

Saul could contain himself no longer. In a burst of anger he leapt to his feet.

'These men are blasphemers! They deserve to die!'

Immediately Gamaliel rose. His voice was calm but he spoke with urgency.

'Men of Israel, take care what you do. I advise you to leave these men alone. For if what they teach comes from men it will die out of its own accord, but if it should spring from God, whatever you may do, you will be unable to put it down. Take care in case you find yourselves fighting against God.'

2
The road to Damascus

IN two years the number of 'Nazarenes' in Jerusalem had increased to thousands. They shared everything they had with each other and some, following the example of Barnabas, sold their land and brought the money to the brotherhood to be distributed among the people according to their needs. Many Jews who had been born abroad had joined them. One of them was a young man called Stephen.

This morning, as usual, the courtyard of Mark's house was filled with people. These were the poor of the city who gathered there each day to be given bread. By the gate stood a group of black-veiled women, the widows. All but one of these got her share of bread and went away. Stephen crossed the courtyard to where the old woman stood alone.

'Why did you not receive any bread, mother?'

Wistfully the woman replied: 'They only give it to the local Jews.'

'Where are you from?'

'From Cilicia. My husband and sons are dead and I came to the homeland to be near my own people. But I am treated as a stranger.'

Stephen pressed some coins into her hand. 'Take this, mother, and buy yourself bread, and tomorrow come here again.'

The woman kissed his hand and with a shy smile of gratitude hurried off down the street. Stephen stood looking after her. Barnabas came up to him, but he hesitated seeing the other so deep in thought. Then Stephen spoke to him: 'They must be fed. *All* the people must be fed.'

When Barnabas and Stephen entered the upstairs room, the twelve were seated, about to have their morning meal. They stood by the door waiting while Peter broke the bread and said the blessing. 'Thanks be to you, Lord, King of the universe, who brings forth bread from the earth.' The bread was handed round and the twelve began talking among themselves. Barnabas stepped forward.

'May I talk to you, Peter?'

Peter smiled a welcome. 'Brother Banabas! Sit down and eat.'

As Barnabas crossed the room and sat down beside him, Peter noticed Stephen standing at the door. 'Who's your friend?' he asked quietly. 'He looks like a foreigner.'

Peter was surprised by the reaction to this question.

'What is a foreigner? I'm from Cyprus. Do you call me a foreigner?'

Feeling that he had somehow offended his friend, Peter was quick to put him at ease. 'I know you are a true son of Israel and a faithful follower of the Lord,' he said with a smile. 'I only meant that your friend looked more like a Greek than a Jew.'

'He is a Jew from Alexandria. There are many like him in the courtyard below and every one of them has been baptized in the name of Jesus.'

Peter was distressed. 'Forgive me, brother, I didn't recognize him. There are so many, so many thousands now. It's hard to know them all.' He called across the table to Stephen. 'Sit down and eat, my brother, you are welcome.'

Andrew and Matthew made room for Stephen and plied him

with food and drink and questions. Relieved, Peter began to
eat. But Barnabas was to disturb him more deeply.

'These I've told you about aren't the only ones, Peter.
Among the thousands you speak of there are hundreds of Jews
from Cilicia, Cyprus, Africa and Asia, even Jews from Rome. . .'

Peter interrupted. 'From Rome? It's spreading like the
master said: "Into all the world".'

'But it isn't working out that way. There's a danger of the
brotherhood becoming a Jerusalem sect.'

Peter was startled by this remark. 'A Jerusalem sect? What do
you mean?'

'Day after day the people from other countries are being
neglected. Their poor don't receive any bread, and their synagogues have no teachers.'

'But why?'

'You yourself thought Stephen there a Gentile.'

Peter understood. He spoke humbly. 'Yes. I'm to blame.
There are only twelve of us, you see, among all these thousands.
Only twelve to baptize and teach and heal the sick. We can't all
leave our work to distribute bread . . . But something must be
done. We mustn't have division among us. We can't have dis-
content. . .' He thought for a moment, then spoke decisively.
'Barnabas, these men you speak of, are there any who would
work for us among their countrymen?'

'I know one who would give his life to spread the news of the
Messiah.' He pointed to where Stephen sat.

Peter knew what he must do. 'Appoint him, and choose six
others among yourselves. We need seven good men who will
work among the Jews from other nations. Gather them
together now, Barnabas, and when you have chosen your men
I'll come and give them the blessing.'

The two men shook hands and Barnabas left the room with
Stephen.

'Peter's right, you know,' said Matthew the ex-tax-collector
who sat on the floor counting the money that had been given.
'It's full-time work just keeping the accounts. So much coming
in.'

'Like being at your old job, Matthew?' asked John with a grin.

Matthew laughed. 'It is, you know, like being a tax-collector again. Only I didn't give any away then!'

In the courtyard below the upstairs room seven men stood waiting. They came from many different countries and all were dressed in the Greek style. But with the exception of one they were all of the Jewish race.

Barnabas came down the stairs with Simon Peter. 'These are the seven we have selected,' he said as he led Peter over to the group. 'Philip ... Prochorus ... Nicanor ... Timor ... Parmenas ... Stephen ...' Peter embraced each man as he would have embraced his brother. '... Nicholas of Antioch ... not born a Jew, but has long been of our faith. ...' Peter hesitated, just for a moment, before embracing the Gentile. Then he told the men to kneel and, placing his hands on each head in turn, he said a blessing. 'Lord, bless this your son, that he may serve you faithfully and feed your people, not only with bread that perishes, but with the true bread of heaven that gives life to the world.'

In the council chamber an informal meeting of the Sanhedrin were sitting. Saul stood facing the high priest who listened to him with unusual patience.

'... The blasphemous teaching of the Nazarenes is spreading through all the synagogues of Jerusalem. Now they have appointed seven men, one of them a Gentile, to bribe the poor with bread and to teach Jews from Rome and Greece and Africa that Jesus the Nazarene was Israel's Messiah.'

'You are an eye-witness?'

'No, my lord, but there are witnesses here.'

With a dramatic gesture of his hand, Saul gave a signal to the guard who stood at the door. All heads turned as the door was flung open and a young man, who had the appearance of a Greek, was dragged in by two others dressed in the same style.

Even Annas was startled. 'Who is this man?'

Saul spoke with triumph. 'A preacher from the Cilician syn-agogue, my lord. He has been heard to speak blasphemous words.'

'What words?'

With another dramatic gesture, Saul commanded one of the captors to speak. He was from North Africa and spoke his native Hebrew with a foreign accent.

'This man said that Jesus the Nazarene would change the law of Moses.'

Saul signalled to the other, who reported:

'I heard him say that Jesus the Nazarene will come again and destroy the holy temple.'

Annas looked at the third man who stood straight and calm between his accusers.

'What is your name?'

'Stephen.'

'You hear what you are accused of. Is it true?'

Instead of replying, Stephen looked round the assembly with a smile, almost of love. He might have been a son who had just returned to his family, instead of a prisoner under the threat of death. Every eye was fixed on him as he stepped forward.

'My brothers and fathers . . .'

There was a rustle of approval at this correct mode of address.

'Before you accuse me of blasphemy, think back over the history of our nation. Where did it begin? Not in the holy temple, not even here in Jerusalem, did it? When God appeared to our ancestor Abraham it was not in this land, but in far off Mesopotamia . . .' Stephen paused for a moment. There was no doubt that he had captured the court's interest. Some were leaning forward staring at him now, with surprise, curious to hear how this unusual captive was going to continue. Stephen noted the interest and knew exactly how he would lead these learned men to the heart of his message. He raised his voice, and spoke as a rabbi might speak to his pupils. 'For 400 years our fathers lived as strangers in a strange land and were treated as slaves. But God had given Abraham a promise. A promise that after the 400 years he would set his descendants free and give them this land where you now live. Four hundred years, my brethren, and at the time of that promise Abraham had no children. But he trusted God. He did not question the covenant that God had made with him. He had no doubt that the promise would be fulfilled. . .'

He paused again to gauge the measure of interest. He was determined not to bore his audience, determined that the desire for more should come from them. It was only a few seconds before the high priest barked:

'Continue.'

Stephen acknowledged the order with a courteous bow of the head. Then, moving from group to group, from priests to Pharisees, from guards to students, he continued his discourse in a friendly tone.

'After Abraham our fathers were not so faithful. You remember how Joseph was sold to slavery in Egypt by his own brothers. But man's wickedness cannot defeat God's purpose. God was with Joseph in Egypt, and that young Jew, sold as a slave, became ruler over the king's household; and it was through him that the Jewish people came to Egypt and multiplied, so that, by the time the 400 years of God's promise were nearly completed, the Jews in Egypt had increased to such an enormous number that the new king Pharaoh was greatly alarmed. He ordered that all Jews were to be persecuted and enslaved and forced to expose their infant children so that the race might die out. Again, it looked like the defeat of God's purpose . . . But it was at this time that Moses was born, a Jewish child of such remarkable beauty that when Pharaoh's daughter found him abandoned, she adopted him and brought him up as her own son. So, while his relatives toiled and suffered as slaves, Moses was trained in all the wisdom of Egypt.'

The council were really absorbed now in this vivid presentation of their history. Stephen knew it was the moment to begin leading them more directly to the point of his discourse.

'But Moses had a great longing to be among his own people,

a great longing to help the children of Israel. So he went down among them, and he found them . . . quarrelling. "You are brothers of the same race," he said, "why do you try to injure each other?" But his fellow-Jews turned on him, saying "Who made you a ruler and a judge over us?" They did not understand, you see, that God had sent Moses to rescue them . . . And so he was rejected by his own people.'

Stephen paused for a moment to let these last words have their effect. The council were still absorbed in his discourse. Not only absorbed, but deeply impressed by his learning and eloquence. But Stephen could not tell yet whether they realized where his words were leading them.

'My brothers and fathers,' he said, addressing the whole court in a strong and vibrant voice. 'You remember what happened next. How this same Moses whom the people of Israel had disowned and cast out was, as Joseph had been before him, sent by God to be their ruler and their saviour. He it was who led them out of Egypt and across the Red Sea, showing by miracles and wonders that the power of God was with him. He it was who said to the children of Israel, "God will send you a prophet, just as he sent me, and he will be one of your own people: *you must listen to him*". He it was who received the living words of God to hand on to us. And yet, our fathers again turned away from him. At the very moment that Moses was receiving the commandments of God, the children of Israel were worshipping a calf made of gold.'

Even though they knew the shameful story so well, some of the older Pharisees were overcome by the remembrances. 'Aie, Aie, Aie,' they wailed and rocked backwards and forwards as Stephen's vibrant voice rose.

'Our ancestors were worshipping an idol they had made with their own hands, even though they had with them the holy tabernacle which now rests here in this temple of Jerusalem. They thought, perhaps, that God lived in that tabernacle. That however often they rejected his chosen leaders, however often they disobeyed his commands, even if they made false gods out of gold, as long as they had the tabernacle they had God.'

The wailing had stopped. Everyone present realized that Stephen had finished speaking of the prophets and was about to speak of the present day. He felt the eager, expectant silence round him. He knew that the moment had come. When he spoke it was with love, as though to brothers of his own flesh and blood.

'My brothers, the Most High God does not live in temples made by men. Remember the words, "Heaven is my throne, and the earth is my footstool. What kind of house, then, could you build for me, what kind of place for me to live in? I myself created the whole universe!" '

Instantly a restless, hostile murmuring spread through the gathering. Saul, in spite of his hatred for this Nazarene, had been as moved as any by his eloquence. But these last words rekindled his hatred and his determination. He sprang to his feet:

'He blasphemes against the temple, my lord.'

But Stephen had not finished. His voice drowned Saul's as he faced the council.

'I tell you, you are hard-hearted and refuse to listen. You are just like your fathers. You always fight against the Holy Spirit. You never recognize the leader God has chosen for you. Which of the prophets did your fathers fail to oppress? ... They persecuted those who foretold the coming of the righteous one. You have betrayed and murdered him.'

The restless whispering became a rumble of anger. Stephen's voice rose and, pointing directly at the council, he delivered his final accusation.

'You, who received the law from the hands of angels and have not kept it.'

The angry voices rose to a clamour. Saul moved quickly to stand between Stephen and the high priest. This time he was determined to be heard:

'He insults you, my lord.'

Annas was held for a moment by the blazing, angry eyes, then he shifted his gaze to the face of the young Nazarene who stood directly behind Saul. He was startled by the contrast.

Stephen's face seemed transfigured. His eyes, calm and happy, looked upwards and beyond the passionate face in front of him. Saul turned round to face the prisoner and signalled to the two witnesses to seize him again. At the same moment Stephen spoke.

'The heavens have opened and I see Jesus standing on the right hand of God.'

No greater blasphemy could have been heard in that court. Annas and the other priests clapped their hands over their ears and a great wail went up. The young men rushed at Stephen with cries of 'Kill him!' 'Death to the blasphemer!' For the first time Annas raised his voice:

'Wait. It is against the law.' Nobody took any notice. Amid shouts and curses Stephen was dragged from the court. Saul turned to the high priest.

'Let me deal with this, my lord.'

Annas nodded and Saul followed the shouting mob.

Stephen was dragged by his captors to the top of a stony hill outside the city and flung down into a shallow pit. Saul stood with the two witnesses. He was in command now. His voice snapped an order:

'Let the witnesses throw the first stone.' The shouting subsided as the two men took off their coats and threw them down at Saul's feet. Then, with a dreadful sort of formality, each picked up a large jagged stone. Saul watched as they hurled the stones down at the man in the pit.

Stephen was on his knees, and although his body was terribly injured, his face was still transfigured with that strange joy, and he spoke in a strong voice as though to a friend who stood near:

'Lord Jesus, receive my spirit.'

Now the stones flew thick and fast until the body in the pit was almost covered. Saul winced as he saw a sharp rock strike the upturned face, and he felt tears behind his eyes as he heard the dying man's voice again:

'Lord, do not hold this sin against them,' and saw the

battered head drop forward on to the stones.

Saul crushed down the sudden surge of pity and his voice was cold as he turned to the man beside him. 'Now for the rest of them.'

That day marked the beginning of the persecution of the church in Jerusalem. The young man Saul took it upon himself to purge the city of the Nazarenes. Some of the disciples escaped to Judea and Samaria, but hundreds of men and women were dragged from their homes and thrown into prison.

The upstairs room, meeting place of the church of Christ, was quiet now. Of the twelve disciples only Simon Peter still stayed in the city, and of the hundreds who had joined the Nazarenes only Barnabas and young John Mark remained.

Peter and Barnabas sat in silence in the room where so much had happened in these last years. The only sound was the swish of Rhoda's broom as she swept the floor. Rhoda was troubled. For weeks now there had been this unnatural silence and this fearful dread that seemed to hang over the room.

Presently she stopped sweeping and went and stood by Peter. He looked up at her anxious little face.

'Master, will they come here?'

Peter shook his head. 'I don't know, Rhoda.'

Rhoda's voice trembled. 'I'm afraid, sir. Every time there's a knock on the gate I think it's them.'

'They've left us alone so far.'

Rhoda crept nearer to him. 'It's so quiet now, isn't it, sir? Just when everything was going so lovely. The crowds and the coming and going, the healing and baptizing and all. And now it's all over.'

Peter took her hand. 'No, Rhoda, it's not over. It's just beginning.'

Rhoda looked at him blankly. 'What?'

'Beginning to spread.'

Barnabas raised his head. 'How do you make that out?'

'Why, think—' Peter seemed to have regained some of his old vigour. 'Think of those who have escaped and carried the

Lord's words to far off places ... you know, I keep remembering something the master said. ... "The forces of death shall never overpower you".'

Suddenly feet were heard running across the courtyard and up the stairs. Rhoda clung to Peter. 'They've come for us.' She stifled a scream as the latch of the door was lifted, but the door was barred. They were safe for the moment. Then came loud urgent knocking. Barnabas signalled to Rhoda. Her knees trembling, she went to the door and called, 'Who is it?'

'It's me, Mark. Open the door.'

But Rhoda was quite unable to do so. At the sound of the familiar voice her legs gave way, and sobbing and laughing with relief she fell on to her knees. Barnabas unbarred the door and Mark burst into the room. He was breathless and his words came in gasps. 'The tyrant Saul has left the city.'

The two men spoke at once.

'The Lord be praised.'

'Where has he gone?'

Relief was short-lived, for Mark's next words brought a new terror.

'He and a company of men are on their way to Damascus. They say he has letters of authority from the high priest to arrest all Jews who speak the name of Jesus and bring them in chains to Jerusalem.'

Despair once more seemed to settle on the room. Peter prayed:

'Lord Jesus be with your disciples in Damascus, especially with your faithful servant Ananias and protect them from the hand of your enemy Saul.'

It was a long journey from Jerusalem to Damascus. But from Galilee onwards the road was a good one, built by the Romans as a trade route to the north. Along this road Saul and his companions rode. At night they camped by the roadside and by day they continued their journey, sometimes riding, sometimes on foot leading their mules. Beyond the mountains the country became more fertile, the heat more intense.

Saul walked ahead, one of his companions leading his mule. The sun beat down upon his head and he marched like a soldier, but his face was that of a sick and haunted man—the eyes fixed and staring, the cheeks drawn and haggard. For Saul was oblivious of his surroundings. Although his feet marched along the burning dusty road, it was the memories of Jerusalem that beat upon his senses. Pictures, terrible pictures danced in front of his eyes and there were voices beating on his ears, beating their way into his brain. Voices of men, of women, of children—

'I believe in Jesus the Messiah . . . Stay near me, Lord Jesus . . . I see Jesus standing at the right hand of God . . . Our Father in Heaven . . . Lord Jesus, receive my spirit . . . Lord, do not hold this sin against them . . .' And then the screams and the mingled voices became one word. One word repeated over and over on a rising crescendo of pain. 'Jesus . . . Jesus . . . Jesus . . . Jesus . . . Jesus.' The marching feet faltered. Saul fell to the ground. Suddenly the voices stopped and then, out of the silence, came a different voice, very quiet and very close. 'Saul . . . Saul, why do you persecute me?'

Slowly Saul raised his head. Brilliant light beat on his eyes and standing in front of him on the sun-drenched road he saw the figure of a man.

'Who are you?'

'I am Jesus. The one you persecute.'

When Saul's companions saw their leader fall they slid from their mules and raced along the road towards him. Then they stopped and stared in amazement. Saul was on his knees, his lips were moving and they heard him say,

'What must I do?'

Only Saul heard the answer.

'Get up now and go into the city and you will be told what you have to do.'

He staggered to his feet and his friends saw him groping about with his hands. They ran up to him.

'Saul—Saul—what's happened?'

His voice was a whisper.

'Lead me to Damascus.'

'Lead—?'

'He's ill.' One of the men looked closely at his face, at the blank staring eyes. 'He's blind!'

They took his hands and led him slowly towards the city. And so, with faltering steps and sightless eyes, Saul the persecutor entered Damascus.

'He's always been a sick man.'

'Didn't seem very sick when we set out.'

'More wine, sirs?'

Judas the innkeeper placed a jug on the table of his distinguished guests from Jerusalem. His was a poor inn, but it was the only one in the city that Jews could enter. It stood on the street called Straight, and he did a fair business when Jewish merchants and traders came to the city. But these men were not traders, and from their conversation he had learned what their business was. He listened more intently.

'That's the way it is with malaria,' said one of the young men, pouring wine. 'Suddenly strikes you and you go out of your mind.'

'Talking to himself there in the road!' said another with a laugh.

'Anyway,' said the first man, 'I've got the high priest's letter. If he doesn't recover soon we'll carry out the plan ourselves.' He looked up and frowned as he noticed Judas hovering near.

'Shall I take something for your friend upstairs, sir?'

'You can try.'

Judas picked up a plate of fruit and some bread from the table and went towards the stairs that led to the upper storey.

'Peace be to you, Judas.'

Judas turned. It was his old friend Ananias. Judas drew him quickly into the shadows and whispered a warning:

'You shouldn't be here, Ananias.'

'I want to speak to Saul of Tarsus.'

'He's ill, lucky for you he is.'

'Take me to him.'

'But he's half dead, can't see or eat or drink.'

'Is that food for him?'

'I was going to leave it by his bed. He's had nothing to eat or drink for three days.'

'Let me take it to him.'

Reluctantly Judas handed the dish to Ananias who took it and went up the stairs.

Saul lay on a mattress on the floor. He looked desperately ill. Though his eyes were open he saw nothing. Only his stiff lips moved as though in prayer. Ananias came quietly into the room. He looked down at the gaunt figure on the bed, then sat down on the floor beside him. Still the blind man remained rigid; unaware that he was not alone. Ananias spoke quietly.

'Saul, my brother.'

The body quivered, the sightless eyes turned towards him, and a whisper came from the parched lips.

'Who are you?'

'My name is Ananias. I have been sent to you by the Lord Jesus.'

'No!' At the name the blind man covered his eyes with his arm and cringed away. 'No—No—No.'

Ananias spoke soothingly as though to a child. 'Ssh. There's nothing to be afraid of.' He had to lean close to the averted face to hear the whisper:

'What am I to do?'

Ananias looked down with compassion at Saul, at the trembling lips, the clenched fist, the tense arm which hid the stricken eyes.

'First,' he said, 'you are to receive your sight again.'

Slowly the arm relaxed. Ananias took the groping hand in both of his as Saul turned again towards him. The trembling had stopped. The face with its hollow cheeks and deep lines of suffering might have been carved out of stone. Yet Ananias could sense the sudden flicker of life behind the graven features, like the tiny bright flame fanned from a quenched fire, and he felt the fire of life in his own body leap up and rush to meet the new-born flame. The old gnarled hands, strong hands of a craftsman, covered the dark unseeing eyes and the two bodies were as one body. A whole body, filled with light.

Saul felt the strong, cool hands on his burning eyes; felt the rekindling of life in his body; felt the horrors that had tormented him slip away and his spirit rise up to meet an overwhelming love. How long the hands covered his eyes he did not know, but suddenly where there had been darkness there was light, and in that light he seemed to see again the face of the man on the Damascus road. As his eyes became used to the light he saw that it was the face of an old man. It was strange, one face seemed to shine through the other as though they were blended together in love and compassion.

'I can see!' It was a cry of joy.

In the courtyard below, Saul's companions were still sitting at their meal. Judas was drawing water from the fountain that stood in the middle of the court. As he turned back towards the house he stared in astonishment. Down the stairs from the upper storey came Ananias, followed by the young man who for three days had been too weak to move. The men at the table looked up.

'Saul!'

Ananias and Saul crossed the courtyard to the fountain.

'Saul!' called one of the men again. There was no answer. The man turned to his companions. 'Who is that man with him?'

'A doctor, I suppose. *Something's* cured him and brought back his sight.'

'Judas, who is that man?'

Judas hesitated. These men were enemies of his old friend. He must be careful.

'His name is Ananias. He is a very devout man and highly respected by all the Jews in Damascus.'

'Is he a doctor?'

'No, he is an olive presser.'

One of the men who had been staring at Ananias and Saul

asked, 'What are they doing at the fountain?'

Judas turned to look.

'Your friend is washing. Ananias seems to be helping him. I expect he is still very weak.'

'Saul of Tarsus,' whispered Ananias, 'I baptize you in the name of Jesus the Messiah.'

So it was that Saul of Tarsus, chief enemy of the disciples of Jesus, who had set out for Damascus to arrest any who used his name, began to preach in the synagogues there that this same Jesus was the Son of God.

King Aretas, the Syrian ruler of Damascus, sat in his courtroom. Motionless on either side of his throne stood his personal bodyguard—two Abyssinian warriors who had been captured and brought to Syria to serve him.

In front of him stood four young Jews from Jerusalem. Aretas had had trouble with Jews, but he had corrected that in the past and now those Jews that lived in Damascus, merchants and craftsmen, were law-abiding citizens and gave no trouble.

One of the young men handed him a parchment scroll. 'This is the letter from the high priest, sir.'

Aretas glanced at it. It was written in Hebrew and in Greek. The Hebrew meant nothing to him, and although he could converse in Greek he read it with difficulty. One name, however, he made out very clearly.

'Your name is Saul of Tarsus?'

'Er—no, your majesty.'

'This letter says that the bearer is a man named Saul of Tarsus. Where is he?'

'He—he was taken ill on the road, sir.'

'Where is he now?'

The Jew hesitated a moment. The king repeated his question.

'I said, where is he now?'

'His illness appears to have driven him mad, sir, and a thing that would seem impossible has happened.'

The king was intensely bored by all this Jewish business.

'*What* has happened?'

'He has turned traitor, sir. He has joined the heretics and is himself preaching in the synagogues that the criminal Jesus . . .'

Aretas, bewildered and irritated, interrupted him—

'What criminal? Who are you talking about now?'

'If you will read the letter, sir.'

With a sigh the king unrolled the scroll again and let his eyes skim over unfamiliar words. . . .

'Disturbance in the synagogues . . . law-breakers . . . dangerous insurrection . . . working in secret to overthrow the rulers . . . blasphemy . . . Jesus . . . the Nazarene . . . the Messiah.'

He looked up 'Is this the criminal you were talking about?'

'Yes, sir.'

'I see, and what does this word "Messiah" mean?'

The reply came after a second's pause:

'The king of the Jews, sir.'

King Aretas was alert at once.

'The *king*? I see. This Jewish sect have a leader whom they wish to make their king. And your friend, emissary of the high priest, has joined the party of this'—he glanced at the letter again—'this Jesus. This is serious. This could mean revolution. You will carry out the orders given in this letter, but first you will arrest Saul of Tarsus and bring him in chains not to Jerusalem, but here to me.'

The young Jew was startled by the sharpness of the king's tone.

'If he should escape, sir?'

'He must not escape!'

'Will your majesty arrange to set guards around the city walls?'

'Guards will be set. But I warn you, if your friend should escape you will be held responsible.'

With a gesture of his hand he dismissed the four young men. Tongue-tied, they bowed their way out. Aretas smiled. These Jews had entered his court with a swagger of self-importance. They had left in fear.

Saul was not at the inn of Judas. They searched every house in the street called Straight until they came to a house built high against the city wall, the house of Ananias the olive presser. They ran up the stairs and burst open the door. The old man and his son were packing the huge jars of olive oil into baskets ready to be picked up by the traders. He looked up in surprise at the four hostile men who confronted him.

'Where is he?'

'Who?'

'Saul of Tarsus.'

'He is not in this house.'

Two of the men pushed by him and searched an inner room. The other began to ransack the workshop, throwing the empty baskets about. They came to three that were covered and strapped down.

'What's in these?' said the leader, giving one of them a kick.

'Olive oil, please take care.'

'Open these baskets.'

Ananias watched them rip the covers off the first two baskets to reveal two large jars of olive oil. One man pulled out a knife and slit the cover of the third basket . . . it too contained a jar of oil.

'He's not here—search the synagogue.'

Ananias followed them to the door and watched them run down the steps. 'All clear.'

His son left his work and crossed swiftly to the large window through which the heavy baskets were lowered to the ground outside the city wall. He hauled on the pulley-rope and dragged into the room one of the large baskets which had been suspended outside. Ananias removed the cover and his son helped Saul climb out. Ananias spoke urgently:

'You must leave the city tonight, brother Saul.'

Saul knew of the search and of the danger, but to leave this friend who had opened his eyes to the truth, to leave him to face the danger?

'But what about you? It was through me that this trouble came to Damascus. You and your boy may be taken in chains to

Jerusalem.'

Ananias was calm and sure. 'There will be more danger if you stay. You are the one who has spoken publicly in the synagogue. There are, as you know, many believers in the city, but we meet privately here at my house. As Jews we are tolerated, but only as long as we make no trouble. In secret we may win all the Jews in Damascus. In public we would be arrested before our work had begun.'

A wave of terrible loneliness swept over Saul. He flung himself into the old man's arms. 'Come with me, come with me to Jerusalem.'

Ananias kissed the young man's forehead. He sensed the loneliness, the sudden fear. As a father with a father's love for the ever-present child in his grown son, he held him in his arms. 'Don't be afraid. Don't worry about me. My work is here. I am well known in the city. I supply the king's palace with oil. Neither the Jews nor the Gentiles can prove anything against me.'

The lonely child was the man of action again. 'Then I must go alone. But how?' He went to the window. 'Guards are all round the walls.'

'When it is dark we will lower you to the ground in this basket,' said the old man. 'No one will suspect. They are used to us working at night.'

At the gate, like black giants, stood two of the Abyssinian guards, spears crossed. And armed guards patrolled the top of the city wall.

Ananias the olive presser was working late, as usual. The traders called at dawn and already there were a dozen or so of the oil-jar baskets lined up against the city wall. Occasionally the guards would stop and watch the baskets descending from the lighted window. It was something to relieve the monotony. But it was a cold night. Too cold to stand still for long. Their cloaks weren't as thick as the fellow's who stood below untying the rope from the baskets as they reached the ground. They did not know that the cloaked fellow was watching them. His moment came. Two guards had passed each other: three minutes he reckoned. He lifted the cover off one of the baskets. Saul climbed out. The man threw his own cloak round Saul's shoulders. They shook hands and Saul slipped off into the night.

3
Simon Peter

IN Jerusalem the disciples that remained still met in the upstairs room of the house of Mary and her son Mark. They had been joined by one of the Lord's own family, another carpenter from Nazareth, James, whom the disciples nicknamed 'The Just'. This evening he and Peter sat talking.

'You know, James,' said Peter, 'what I can't get over is all that time we were in Galilee with the master, yet never met you.'

James was the soul of honesty. 'I purposely kept away. You see, I didn't want to be mixed up with Jesus and what he was doing. You know how it is in a family if one of the members starts drawing attention to himself and putting forward new-fangled ideas, the others tend to draw away from him. Sort of embarrassed!'

'Ashamed?'

'Yes, even ashamed.'

'And what changed you?'

James hesitated before answering. Then, looking at Peter's humble, compassionate face, he remembered how much of his own experience the other had shared and knew that here was the man who might understand.

'It was after he was crucified. That was a terrible shock. I never thought it would come to that, and of course I was more ashamed than ever to belong to the same family. It seemed like the final disgrace . . .'

Peter nodded, remembering the arrest in the garden, the courtyard outside the trial chamber. He knew how shame and fear made even those who loved most dearly forsake their friend when he became a prisoner. There was silence for a moment, then James spoke again:

'And then, one day soon after, I was in the shop planing a piece of wood when I felt someone standing beside me. I looked up and it was him. Jesus . . . Well, you can imagine what I felt.'

Peter knew. 'Afraid.'

'Paralysed with fright. Thought it was a ghost. Then he began to talk to me about the work I was doing, and gradually the strangeness and the fear changed to something close and familiar, as though we were boys again, working in the shop together. I began to think I was asleep and dreaming . . . And that's what I told myself in the days that followed. It was a dream; and I tried to put it out of my mind . . . Then all that persecution started against you people and it seemed . . . well, as though they were trying to crucify him all over again: and I made up my mind that this time I'd throw in my lot on the right side.'

Peter leant across and put his hand over his new friend's. 'We're glad to have you with us, James. There's not many of us left in the city.'

'What became of that man, Saul of Tarsus, who started all the trouble?'

'Last we heard of him he was going up to Damascus. But he's never brought any prisoners back, or we'd have heard.'

Peter turned to speak to Mark who stood at the window.

'Any sign of Barnabas?'

'No. I wish he would come.'

Peter sensed the strain behind Mark's words.

'He'll come.' Mark sighed. 'What's troubling you, boy?'

'I want to ask him something.'

Peter looked at the boy's set face. 'Something so serious?' he asked with a smile.

Mark turned. 'I think it's serious.' Then, drawn by the warmth and kindliness in Peter's eyes, he came and stood beside him.

'You remember last week when Philip was here . . .?'

Peter nodded. Philip was one of the apostles who had been doing great work in the south.

'Well, he told us that one of the people he baptized was a Gentile.'

James looked from Mark to Peter in complete amazement.

'A *Gentile?*'

'That's right,' said Peter, 'an Ethiopian. Philip met him in Gaza.'

Mark turned to James.

'It seems that this fellow was reading from our scriptures,' he explained, 'and he asked Philip about some words of the prophet Isaiah.'

'These were the words,' said Peter. ' "Like a sheep that is taken to be slaughtered, like a lamb that makes no sound when its wool is cut off, he did not say a word." . . . He asked Philip who the words referred to, so Philip told him about our Lord, and the man asked to be baptized.'

'But should he have done that, Peter?' Mark's voice was troubled.

'How could he refuse?' said Peter. 'It would be like refusing a cup of water to a thirsty man.'

'But the man wasn't a Jew,' protested Mark. 'How could he understand?'

'Because he *wanted* to understand.' Peter's eyes shone as he remembered. 'Like the master said, "Happy are those whose greatest desire is to do what God requires; God will satisfy them fully."'

Mark turned back to the window, unconvinced. James too was troubled.

'It's a big step, Peter, to accept Gentiles.'

'A step forward, perhaps.'

They were interrupted by a joyful shout from Mark.

'Here's Uncle Barnabas! And there's someone with him . . . looks like a beggar.'

Peter rose.

'Barnabas will be bringing him up for food. Fetch bread and wine, Mark.'

'No, he's left him in the courtyard. He's coming up alone.'

Peter crossed to the window as Mark rushed to the door to welcome his uncle. The tall figure of Barnabas appeared in the doorway. He embraced Mark warmly and greeted the other two, but he did not enter the room.

'Who's your friend outside, Barnabas?' said Peter from the window.

He did not reply at once. Three pairs of eyes looked at him questioningly. Then, looking straight at Peter, he said very gravely:

'Saul of Tarsus.'

The name filled the room with an almost forgotten terror. James leapt to his feet, Mark's joy in his uncle's return was swallowed up in fear. Peter felt the cold fingers of panic clutching his heart. He struggled to keep his voice steady.

'Saul!'

'I found him in the street, ill and ragged. I didn't recognize him at first. He has a strange story to tell.'

The icy fingers were pressing against Peter's temples, squeezing the life from his brain. A cold mist seemed to cloud his eyes as he gazed into the face of Barnabas, praying that the burning hope he read there might kindle in him. The voices in the room sounded distant.

'It's a trap.'

'He's ill.'

'Drive him away.'

'He's hungry.'

'Lock the doors.'

'He's asking to see you, Peter.'

'Peter, Peter, what are you going to do?'

Suddenly his memory rang with another voice:

'I was hungry and you took me in . . . Naked and you clothed me. . . Anything as you do for one of these . . .'

The mist cleared. Warmth flooded his body. He was aware of his three friends looking earnestly at him. Appealing to him. Awaiting his answer.

His voice was steady now. 'Bring him up, Barnabas.'

They watched from the window as Barnabas crossed the courtyard to the ragged man who sat huddled against the wall.

'Suppose it's a trap,' murmured James. 'What if all the trouble starts up again?'

Peter's fear had left him, he spoke as the leader, the shepherd of his flock.

'We must risk that. This man has come to us as a beggar. Did our Lord ever refuse to show love and mercy to a beggar?'

It was dark now. Peter lit the lamp while the others watched in silence the two shadowy figures move across the courtyard to the steps. They turned to the door, listening as the footsteps climbed to the upstairs room.

And then he was standing there in the lamplight, Saul the beggar. James was surprised to see so small a man. Small, dirty, emaciated, his hair and beard white with dust. The hands clutching his ragged cloak seemed to have no more flesh on them than the claws of a bird. Was this the tyrant? But it was the eyes that Mark noticed. They had been closed for a moment against the sudden light. Then they opened and it was as though two great fires had been lit in the room. Mark had never seen such eyes: burning, searching, devouring, and yet there was peace in them and, strangest of all, love. He felt his heart beating with a new excitement, an excitement that held no fear.

Peter crossed straight to the man in the doorway and took his hands.

'Peace be with you, friend.'

He led Saul to a couch, knelt at his feet to undo the sandals, then poured clean water from a pitcher over the bruised and dirty feet.

'You wash my feet?' There was shame, entreaty and wonder in the cracked voice.

'It's what our master would have done. He washed my feet here in this room.'

Saul's eyes, those burning, devouring eyes, travelled round the room.

'Is this the room where Jesus stayed?'

'Yes,' said Peter as he dried the weary feet. 'We ate our last supper together here.' He glanced up at the other's face, then continued in the same homely tone. 'And it was here that he first came to us when he had risen from the dead.' There was no sign from Saul of Tarsus, only a horrified gasp from James at these dangerous words, and as Peter rose to put the pitcher away he could contain his anxiety no longer. He strode over to Saul.

'Why have you come to us?'

Saul raised his eyes to meet the other's.

'Because I too have seen him.'

The three disciples stared at their visitor as though he was out of his mind.

'*You* have seen the Lord?' said Peter, kneeling by his feet again.

'Seen him and heard his voice.'

'Where?'

'On the road to Damascus.'

And sitting there in the upstairs room Saul of Tarsus told his strange story to the apostles of Jesus.

But Saul, the apostle of Christ, was almost as great a danger to the brotherhood as Saul the persecutor. News of his return to Jerusalem soon spread for, as in Damascus, he spoke public-ly in the synagogues of the truth that had been revealed to him 'That Jesus who was crucified is the son of the Most High God.' It seemed to the brotherhood as though he was wanting to atone for the death of Stephen and ran the risk of a similar fate. They were all aware of the danger, but it was James of Nazareth who put it into words. He and Peter were alone in the upstairs room. Peter was gathering a few things together in a bundle, for he was off to Joppa the next day. James paced restlessly about the room.

'You don't mind being left in charge here do you, James?'

'There's only one thing that worries me,' said James, coming over to help tie the bundle. 'This man Saul...'

'Ah!' Peter could understand.

'Oh, I don't doubt his sincerity, but in my opinion he's going about things the wrong way. All this public speaking in the synagogues ... that's what started the trouble before.'

'I know, I know,' agreed Peter. 'I was surprised myself.' He chuckled as he added, 'But then he's a surprising sort of fellow.'

'I wish you could persuade him to go with you. After all, he's a lot to learn about the brotherhood. It would help him to see you at work.'

'I wonder? ... Ah no, he'll be better here. Barnabas will keep an eye on him.'

As he spoke the door opened and the two they had been talking of came in without a word. Saul walked to the far end of the room and sat alone, his head in his hands. Peter looked at Barnabas. 'What happened?' he asked quietly.

'They wouldn't let him speak,' said Barnabas in shocked tones.

'Where?'

'In the Cilician synagogue. Some of our brothers were there. They were afraid to be seen talking to him.'

'Why were they afraid?'

'They say some men have reported Saul to the high priest. They're afraid the persecutions will start again.'

James joined them. He too spoke quietly, but with urgency.

'And he'll be the first victim. We must get him away, Peter.'

Peter looked at the silent, bowed figure and went over to him.

'Saul.'

'Yes.'

'I'm leaving the city today. Going down to the coast. Why don't you come with me?'

Staring at the floor, Saul spoke as though to himself in a

voice that was flat and dead.

'I thought they'd be bound to listen to me. Bound to believe me. They know what I was before.'

'That's why they want to get rid of you,' said Peter gently. 'A turn-coat, a traitor. That's what they think.'

At last Saul raised his head and looked at Peter.

'You want me to run away?'

'They'll kill you if you stay here.'

'They'll kill us all,' said James.

Wearily Saul got to his feet and appealed to his closest friend.

'What am I to do, Barnabas?'

'There's only one thing for you to do,' persisted James, suddenly assuming command, 'Leave the city today. Tomorrow may be too late.'

'Barnabas?' It was a cry for help. Not for nothing was Joseph Barnabas nicknamed 'the son of consolation'.

'We'll both go. We'll travel with Peter as far as Joppa and then on to Cæsarea. From there we could get a ship to Cyprus, or even to your home-town, Tarsus. Peter'll send for us when this trouble's blown over.'

Saul looked at Peter appealingly. 'But what about the work?'

'There'll be plenty of work for you to do. You'll see.'

In Joppa, Simon the Tanner lived in a small, flat-roofed house by the sea. On the roof and among the skins stretched to dry on the white walls hung the fishing nets of his guest, Simon Peter.

It was noon and Peter was resting on the roof. After his morning's fishing he was hungry. He leaned over and called:

'Simon, is the meal ready?'

Simon came out of the house carrying a skin.

'Not yet, I'm waiting for the fish to cook.'

'Isn't there anything else to eat? I'm hungry.'

'Not unless you want pork,' called Simon as he stretched the skin out on the wall.

'Pork!' Peter was shocked. To a Jew pork was unclean meat.

'That's right,' said Simon with a chuckle. 'From this pigskin I'm drying.'

Peter laughed. 'You'd better be careful what you say—you'll be taken seriously one of these days. Pork indeed! I'm going to have a sleep. Call me when the fish is ready,' and after saying his prayers he settled down to sleep under the shade of his drying nets. There was a light breeze flapping the net over his head. He closed his eyes and though his hunger prevented him from falling into a deep sleep, in his drowsy mind the billowing net and Simon's joke about the pork formed themselves into a strange dream. The net over his head became heavy as though filled with a good day's catch, but when it was lowered to the ground beside him he saw in it not only fish, but all the creatures of the earth—birds—reptiles—animals of every kind. As he lay looking at these creatures, suddenly through his dream he heard a voice:

'Get up, Peter—kill and eat.'

'No—no—.' Peter spoke aloud. 'I've never eaten anything ritually unclean.'

Then the voice spoke again.

'Do not consider anything unclean that God has declared clean.'

These words were ringing in his ears when he awoke. From below he heard the sound of horses' hoofs, then a voice asking for him by name. He rose quickly and ran down the steps. Three men stood by the door. One of them, a Roman soldier, was talking to Simon.

'I'm the man you're looking for,' said Peter. 'Why have you come?'

The young soldier looked relieved. His search was ended.

'You are Simon called Peter?'

'Yes.'

'Sir, the Centurion Cornelius, officer of the Italian regiment stationed at Cæsarea, sends you greetings. He asks that you return with us to his house in Cæsarea.'

For a moment Peter was startled. He was being asked to go with a pagan to visit a pagan household. The soldier noticed his hesitation.

'The centurion was most anxious, sir. He says that you have

something to tell him.'

And in a flash Peter saw the meaning of his strange dream. This stranger was one of God's creatures. It was not for Peter the Jew to reject him because he belonged to a different race. He held out his hand to the soldier.

'Come inside, my son, you and your friends must rest and eat. Tomorrow I'll come with you to Cæsarea.'

On a hillside above the busy harbour of Cæsarea stood a Roman villa; the Centurion Cornelius was at the window, his eyes scanning the straight coastal road that led from Joppa to the north. Behind him, in the room, his family and all his household servants were gathered together.

'Here they come!'

The excitement in the centurion's voice was reflected in the faces of the others as he turned and ran from the room. He stood at the gate until they had dismounted, the soldier, his two servants, and the man they had brought from Joppa. Then he ran forward and knelt at Simon Peter's feet.

'Stand up,' said Peter. 'You mustn't kneel to me. I'm a man like yourself.'

Cornelius rose and taking hold of Peter's hand he led him towards the house. 'All my family are waiting for you,' he said, and then, remembering that this man was a Jew, he paused and looked at him searchingly. 'You will come in, won't you?'

Peter didn't hesitate this time. 'Yes,' he said with a smile, 'I'll come in.'

The family watched in silence as Cornelius led his guest into the room. The servants washed his feet and brought him food and water, and when he was comfortably settled Cornelius introduced his family and trusted servants. Peter smiled round at the eager, expectant faces, then turned to his host.

'Now tell me, friend, what made you send for me?'

'Before I answer you,' said Cornelius, 'I want you to know that for many years now I and my family have worshipped the one true God. Though not of your race, nor circumcised according to your custom, we have fasted and prayed and given charity to those in need as taught by the rabbis of your faith.'

'I know,' said Peter. 'Your servants told me on the way.'

Cornelius sat beside him. 'But lately,' he said, 'I have been filled with a strange sense of longing. More than that, an absolute conviction that something was missing, or rather that there was something very close to me, yet out of reach. It was as if my whole nature, body, heart and mind, was straining towards a great truth, and yet there was a veil between that truth and me. Each day I fasted until three in the afternoon, and then I prayed that God would open my eyes to this mystery, which I knew to be the secret of life itself.'

He hesitated. Peter felt his own heart beat with excitement.

'Go on.'

'I'm a soldier, sir. Not a man given to dreams or strange fancies, and there are not many men who would believe what I have to tell you now.'

'I will believe you.'

'Four days ago I was praying here as usual, when suddenly I saw a man standing there in front of me. He was dressed in white clothes, and a light seemed to shine all around him. I stared at him, not daring to speak in case he should vanish. You see, this was no ordinary man like you and me. He looked like . . .' the soldier faltered. 'Well, like an angel. Then he spoke to me. He said, "Cornelius, your prayers have been heard. Send to Joppa and ask that a man called Simon Peter be brought to you. . ."' The soldier searched Peter's face, wondering if he did indeed believe this strange story. He was tongue-tied for a moment, a little shy at having talked with such unaccustomed eloquence. When he continued it was in a more matter-of-fact voice. 'I lost no time in sending for you, sir, and you have done me a great favour by coming so far. Will you, in the presence of your God and mine, tell us the good news you have brought?'

Peter felt a great rush of love and gratitude. His voice was warm and humble.

'It's like a fresh wind from heaven to hear you talk. You've taught me something. I see now that God makes no distinction between men of different races, but will pour himself into the heart of any man who truly loves and serves him.'

He looked once more at the silent, expectant faces round him.

'I will tell you what you want to know. . . Do you remember a time, a few years ago, when a story was spreading over all Judea about a man from Nazareth in Galilee who went about doing good, making the lame walk, the blind see, and healing those who were mentally ill?'

'Why, yes,' said Cornelius with interest. 'It must be the same man a fellow officer of mine met when he was serving in Capernaum. I remember he was full of it at the time. It seems that a servant of his, a lad he'd reared from boyhood and was fond of, picked up a fever there. Most of the household gave him up for dead, but my friend had heard that there was a Jewish healer in the district and ran himself to find him. The lad was cured from that moment. So the story goes.'

Peter was carried back over the years and saw himself standing beside his master on the dusty road.

'The centurion in Capernaum,' he murmured. 'I remember that day clearly.'

'Were *you* there?'

'I used to be a fisherman on Lake Galilee. My home was close to Capernaum.'

'Then you knew this man, this healer? What was his name?'

'Jesus of Nazareth. I was with him when your friend came running along the road towards us. We thought it meant trouble. You don't often see a Roman officer running! He ran straight up to Jesus and told him about this servant of his who was so desperately ill. Jesus offered to go with him to his house, but the centurion said there was no need. If Jesus would just say the word he knew that the sickness would leave the young man.'

'It did. He told me so. He had great faith in this . . . this Jesus.'

'Yes, great faith. I can remember the Lord's words about him. "I have not found faith like this in Israel".'

Cornelius was puzzled. 'You called him "Lord"?'

'Yes.'

'But I thought that a Jew wouldn't call any man "lord". Isn't that so? Only God is Lord?'

'But we also call the Messiah Lord.'

'You mean the "Christ", the holy one whom you believe God will send to deliver your people?'

'Yes.'

With rising excitement he asked, 'Where is he now?'

Peter was silent.

'Where is he, this Jesus of Nazareth whom you call Lord?'

For a moment Peter's courage seemed to waver. How could be begin to tell the amazing truth to this honest, God-fearing soldier? He prayed for help while the question stood between them like a cup waiting to be filled. At last he spoke.

'Didn't you hear what happened to him?'

'No, I never heard of him again after that incident in Capernaum.'

'He was crucified.'

Peter saw the hope fade from his new friend's eyes, as though the empty cup had been knocked from his hand. His voice was harsh as he asked:

'What had he done?'

'He travelled around doing good.'

'There must be more to it than that. Roman law is just. We wouldn't arrest a man for preaching and healing, let alone crucify him.'

'He was not arrested by your soldiers, but by his own people.'

'By the Jews? But why, what had he done?'

'The accusation was that he had called himself "the Son of God".'

Again Cornelius was deeply puzzled and a little impatient now.

'Doesn't your faith teach that God is the Father of all men? What is the crime, then, in a man calling himself a son of God?'

'Among our people the words have become to mean the Messiah.'

'So it was a charge of blasphemy?'

'Yes.'

'I see. But, forgive me, blasphemy may be a crime according to Jewish law, but a Roman court would not sentence a man to death for it. A Roman court wouldn't know what it meant. And the Jews have no power to crucify.'

'That is true. But if the council of the Sanhedrin, that is the highest Jewish court, find a man guilty of blasphemy or any other crime, which in their law deserves the death penalty, then they present him to the governor and demand . . . that justice shall be done.'

'Justice?' the soldier's voice was stern. 'Do you mean to say that the governor, Pilate wasn't it, condemned this man to be crucified on a charge of blasphemy?'

'Not entirely. The priests had thought of that, you see. So they told Pilate that Jesus had been telling the people not to pay tribute to Cæsar and that he had called himself "The king of the Jews".'

'I see. And had he?'

It was as though he, Simon Peter, was on trial. He prayed that he might be a faithful witness, and though his heart ached with the pain of remembering, his voice was steady.

'He never called himself a king, though some of the people who heard him speak and witnessed the miracles that he did, addressed him as "king of Israel".'

'And what about the other charge, paying tribute to Cæsar?'

'I can tell you what he said about that. I was in the temple with him when one of the Pharisees who disapproved of his teaching and wanted to trap him, asked him whether he thought it was lawful for Jews to pay tribute to Cæsar. Jesus didn't answer him directly. He did what he so often did, he made the man find the answer himself.'

'How?'

'He asked the man to bring him a coin. When he did so Jesus asked him whose head he saw engraved on the coin. When the man told him it was Cæsar's, Jesus said to him, "Then give to Cæsar the things that are Cæsar's, and to God the things that are God's".'

For the first time since the bitter blow to his rising hopes Cornelius smiled.

'That was a good answer. A clever answer. Did they tell Pilate that?'

'No, they brought false witnesses.'

Relentlessly the questions went on.

'Who did, your people or mine?'

'My people.'

'But what about you and his other followers? I take it you were one of his—what do they call it?—one of his disciples?'

'One of the first.'

'Well then, couldn't you have spoken for him. Like you're speaking for him now. Couldn't you?'

Now it was coming out. The memory that haunted him.

'All his disciples deserted him.'

'You too?' It was a gasp of disbelief.

'I was the worst. I denied that I knew him.'

Cornelius read the agony on the other's face, the tears of shame that misted his eyes, but he could not stop his questioning now. He must know the whole story.

'But why?' he asked gently, echoing the question that had haunted Peter ever since that dreadful night. He knew the answer, but he could not speak.

'You were afraid?'

Peter nodded.

There was one more question that had to be asked.

'Did you believe that he was the Christ?'

Peter raised his head and at the same time lifted his spirit above the shame and pain. The news he had brought was not of a dead friend, but of the living Christ. Warmth flooded his voice as he answered:

'When we were working together, and there was a lot of work, we didn't seem to think so much of the glory of God that was in him. You see, we were a group of friends—that's what he said himself: "You are my friends"—and it was down to earth work in a way, feeding the hungry, healing the sick, telling poor sinners about the love of God, resisting opposition, because opposition grew as the following grew. It was hard work, too, day after day after day, and we loved it because we loved our friend. But one day. . .' Peter paused. The centurion held his breath. 'One day three of us had gone up in the mountains with him to pray. He liked to be high up and alone sometimes, and he had gone ahead of us. Suddenly, as I looked at him it seemed—I think you'll understand this—it seemed as though the glory of God shone all around him. And I *knew* . . . that he was the Christ, Son of the living God.'

The glory of that day shone from Peter's eyes as he remembered. Nobody in that room could have doubted the absolute truth that lay behind the simple statement. To Cornelius it was the bitterest moment of his life. Was this the 'good news' he had been promised? He could have struck the man who brought it him. His voice was harsh.

'We crucified God's Christ. Is that what you have come to tell me? Jews and Gentiles between us, we killed our Saviour?'

'Yes.'

Cornelius buried his head in his hands. Peter looked at him with compassion. This was the way it had to be told—the way of life itself—through agony to resurrection.

'But that wasn't the end of the story.'

The stricken face was raised to him.

'Cornelius, Jesus is alive.'

'But you said . . .?'

'He was crucified, dead and buried. I helped to carry his body to the tomb. Three days later the tomb was empty.'

'The body was stolen?'

'No. Jesus came back to life. Our sin killed him. His goodness, the goodness of God brought him back to us alive.'

'You have seen him?' It was a whisper.

'Yes, I have seen him.'

'A vision?'

'No, it was no vision. It was the Lord himself. Our friend and master as we knew him, a man of flesh and bones. But there was a difference. He had the marks of the nails in his hands. He had supper with us in the very room where we had eaten together on the night of his arrest. And after supper he told us what we were to do.'

'Yes?'

'He said: "You are my witnesses. I hand over to you the message of the Father. Go out into every part of the world telling people of every nation the things that you have seen and heard. Baptize them in my name and teach them the things that I have taught you. And remember, I am with you always, even to the end of the world".'

The glory that had shone from Peter's eyes seemed to fill the room. Cornelius sprang to his feet, his face transfigured. His voice a shout of joy.

'So that's it. He is with us. The Son of the living God.' And falling on his knees he called out, 'Jesus—Lord—everything I have belongs to you.'

Peter watched, deeply moved, as the family and servants took up the cry and the room rang with the name of Jesus. Some words of his master echoed in his memory, 'Because you have seen me you have believed. How happy are those who have not seen me and yet believe.'

'Peter, is this true what we hear? Is it true that you stayed in the house of an Italian soldier in Cæsarea and that you baptized his family?'

The speaker was James of Nazareth. A stickler for the law, he was deeply shocked by Peter's action. Peter had expected this. He sat down among his friends in the upstairs room in Jerusalem and told them the story of his strange dream in Joppa, of the Lord's words, 'It is not for you to call anything that God has made unclean', and of his experience in the Roman house.

Only young Mark still harboured some doubt.

'But why did you baptize them?'

'How could I refuse to baptize men who were filled with the Holy Spirit?'

There was a gasp of astonishment from the disciples.

'It's true,' said Peter. 'As true as it was in this room on the day of Pentecost. Everyone in that soldier's household felt the presence of the living Christ. There was no doubt. I couldn't mistake a thing like that. Then I remembered what the master said to us, "John baptized with water, but you will be baptized with the Holy Spirit". You ask me why I baptized them in the name of Jesus. Who am I to try to hold God back?'

'But what about the Law?' asked young Mark. 'God's words to Abraham, to Moses? What will become of us if we begin to turn away from the Law? Where will it end?'

Peter smiled at the boy.

'The end is in God's hands, lad. None of us knows what it will be. That's something the master never told us.'

4
Herod
the king

ALL through Judea, Galilee and Samaria, the church of Christ grew in numbers and enjoyed peace. Those who had scattered after the persecutions had carried the news of Jesus the Messiah as far as Phœnicia, Cyprus and Antioch. But at the time that Claudius was Emperor of Rome a great famine spread over the eastern countries. In Jerusalem people were starving on the streets, and when it was discovered that King Herod was in the city hungry crowds gathered at the palace gates, for the king held control of the food supplies of Judea and the surrounding districts.

Herod Agrippa I was a puppet king, responsible to the Roman governor for order in the Jewish nation, yet without any real authority. Educated in Rome, he had abandoned the religion of his ancestors and tried in his dress and manner to imitate the Roman rulers whom he greatly admired. For this he was despised by his own people and openly criticized by the religious leaders, the Pharisees. His unpopularity was a gnawing worry at the back of his arrogance. Sometimes it made him really afraid.

Today, he reclined on his balcony listening with irritation to the pitiful cries which floated up to him through the fetid summer air.

'There's a smell of death. Everywhere a smell of death.'

A slave broke open a jar of precious ointment. He held it to his nostrils. A priest, one of the Sadducees, whom Herod employed as his 'religious adviser', was looking down at the crowds below. Herod addressed him petulantly while the slave anointed his forehead: 'Why should the Lord God see fit to strike my lands with famine? Can you answer me that, my lord priest?'

The priest turned. He spoke smoothly. 'The Lord God moves in a mysterious way, your majesty. Famine, earthquake, plague, invasion; they come and go. But in the end the order of life is not greatly disturbed.'

'The order of life for you and me, perhaps,' said the king, taking a sweetmeat from a dish beside him and holding it up between his fingers. 'Gifts from princes and governors do not come the way of every man. You are privileged, my lord priest.'

The priest bowed with a trace of mockery. His position was assured. Herod munched the sweet and then gave a sigh of self-pity.

'I shall be blamed by the people. You'll see. The ignorant will think I am stealing their food. The Pharisees will call it God's judgement on my wickedness. None of you realize the difficulty and the loneliness of your king. I wish the people of Judea had one half of the loyalty and love that the Gentiles show to their emperor. Cæsar is worshipped. By law he is worshipped. . .', he inhaled the heavy scent of the ointment, '. . . like a god.'

Even the worldly Sadducee was shocked. 'Your majesty!'

'I know, I know. "Worship the Lord your God and serve only him".' He gabbled the text like a peevish child, then, leaning his anointed head on the silk cushions, he spoke pensively: 'But there was once a Jew who was worshipped as a god. I heard my uncle Antipas speak of him. Not so long ago either, in your time I should say. Just a peasant, from Galilee I believe, but possessed of some powers of magic or hypnotism or something. Anyway, it brought the people running to him. Did you ever come across him?'

'Yes,' said his adviser dryly, 'I was a member of the court that tried him for blasphemy.'

'Blasphemy. Yes, there is that, of course.' He sighed. 'They don't last long, these mad Messiahs. Between the priests and the Romans, they're caught in a trap. All the same he did have his moment of glory.'

Suddenly the voices outside grew louder as the sound of horses and chariot wheels approached the palace. The priest looked over the balcony again.

'Here comes your son.'

The change in King Herod was extraordinary. Vanity and petulance vanished from his face, to be replaced by an expression of the tenderest love. He sprang to his feet with surprising agility and crossed swiftly to stand beside the priest, to catch the first glimpse of his beloved son. Prince Agrippa, like his father had been, was being educated in Rome. He lived at the court of the emperor and was returning to his own land for a holiday. As the chariot rolled through the palace gates the cries grew louder still:

'Bread. Give us bread. Son of Herod, plead for us. Our children are starving. Bread . . . bread . . . bread.'

For a moment Herod's face clouded.

'Bread. Your magician from Galilee would have turned the stones to bread for them.'

His mood lifted again as the Princess Berenice burst into the room.

'He's come, father, he's come. I saw the chariot from my balcony. There's a huge crowd at the gate to welcome him. All shouting and waving their arms.'

The king kissed her, sharing her excitement, then stepped back to admire his pretty, lively daughter.

'You look beautiful.'

'Will he think so?' The young princess adored her elder brother.

Before Herod could answer there was an announcement.

'Prince Agrippa, your majesty,' and Blastus, the king's

chamberlain, ushered into the room a tall, handsome young man, dark and Asiatic in feature, but in dress and bearing a young Roman.

'My son!' Herod held out his arms.

'Abba!' In his emotion the Hebrew word of his childhood came to the boy's lips as he embraced his father. His eyes shining with pride and love, the king held his son at arm's length, taking in his splendid growth, his princely bearing.

'My boy is a man. Such clothes, such bearing. Like a young emperor, you look.'

'Do I really?' He paraded in front of them, showing off his clothes and his muscles. 'Like a real Roman?'

Then he noticed his sister, who was ready to dance with excitement and impatience.

'Little Berenice!'

She ran into his arms then stood back, posing. It was her turn to be admired.

'But you've grown up. You're beautiful.'

'Like an empress?'

'Like a goddess!'

Herod joined in the laughter, and, putting an arm round each of his children, he led them to the balcony. Agrippa sank down on the couch, while a slave came forward with water and washed his feet.

'Phew! What a journey. I'd heard there was famine, but I'd no idea it was so bad.'

'My boy is hungry?'

'No, I'm not hungry. We brought provisions from Italy. Plenty for the palace, too. I felt bad, I can tell you, driving through the country, well fed and with a camel train of provisions.'

'Bad, why bad?' asked Berenice, sitting at her brother's feet and leaning her head against his knees.

'Because the people are starving to death, little sister; women and children dying in the fields, while they try to scratch in the earth for a root or a grain of wheat. I should have given them what I'd brought, I suppose.'

'No, no, my son.' Herod could not bear either of his children to be distressed. 'Whatever you brought, however much, would have been no more than a handful of grain among so many. To feed just a few of the people would be of no use.'

But the young prince would not be comforted.

'It was worst outside the palace gates. There was a huge crowd collected there, and when my chariot drove through they began to shout. . .'

'I heard them,' said Berenice gaily. 'They were cheering and shouting because you had come here.'

'Oh, no. They shouted, "Give us bread, son of Herod, give us bread".' He leant back with a sigh as the slave bathed his forehead, 'I wish I had given it to them.'

The princess jumped to her feet, determined to change the sudden sad mood that was spoiling her brother's homecoming. She stamped her foot with mock childishness.

'You seem to care more about those people out there than about your own family!' She snuggled down beside him on the couch. 'Didn't you bring me anything from Rome?'

As she had hoped, Agrippa responded to her mood.

'Yes, I did, I was forgetting.' He put an arm round his sister. 'For you, and for father.' He turned to the chamberlain. 'Blastus, where are the gifts I brought?'

'I'll fetch them, sir.'

The cries from below had stopped. Agrippa, drawn by the sudden silence, rose and looked over the balustrade. The crowd was still there, but now two men moved among them carrying baskets of bread.

'There are some men there giving out food to the people.' He turned to his father eagerly. 'Did you send them, father?'

Herod came and stood beside his son.

'Blastus may have given orders as a token of your homecoming. He's a clever fellow for doing the right thing at the right time. . .'

At this moment Blastus returned, carrying a large basket. He placed it on the couch beside Berenice. She lifted the lid and with a squeal of delight lifted out a magnificent silk shawl interwoven with gold and silver. She draped the shawl over her head. Her brother beamed at her and said with pride:

'It's like the ladies at the emperor's court wear.' He went to the basket and took out another richly woven garment. 'For you, father. A present from Claudius himself.'

Herod flushed with pleasure as he handled the emperor's gift.

'Put it on, father. Put it on now,' begged his daughter.

It needed no more persuasion and within a minute he was standing before them in a Roman toga of royal purple clasped with a golden eagle. His children laughed delightedly.

'Hail Cæsar! Hail Cæsar!' shouted Agrippa, and raised his arm in a royal salute.

The gay mood had returned. The famine was forgotten. But the mock Roman ceremony was interrupted by the hurried entrance of the priest:

'Your majesty . . . the people at the gates . . . listen.'

The laughter stopped and from below came the sound of singing.

'What is it?' said Herod. 'A hymn of welcome for my son?'

'No, sir, it is not.' Startled by the urgency of his tone, Blastus crossed quickly to the balustrade and looked down at the crowds. Herod stroked his silken robe.

'Well at least they are not crying "Give us bread" any more. Was it you that fed them, Blastus?'

The chamberlain turned, startled.

'Fed them? No, sir. Your orders were to guard the stores and give none to the people.'

Agrippa looked sharply at his father, who avoided his eye.

'I thought I could count on you to use your own discretion, Blastus,' he said. 'It would have been a good gesture. A popular gesture.'

The chamberlain flushed. Agrippa turned to the priest.

'Somebody fed them. Who was it?'

'The Nazarenes.'

All Herod's petulance and irritability had returned. He was

furious with his two ministers for somehow discrediting him in
his son's eyes.

'*Nazarenes?* What are you talking about? Do you mean
Nazar*ites?* I thought they were a sect who lived in the desert
and starved themselves.'

'Your majesty must have heard of the Nazarenes. You were
talking about their leader only a short while ago. The miracle
worker from Nazareth in Gaililee.'

'You told me that man was dead.'

Blastus, the diplomat, intervened. As a Roman, Herod
listened to him with more sympathy than to the priest. Here
was a chance to reassert himself after the reproof about the
food.

'Jesus of Nazareth was crucified some years ago, your majesty, but from time to time his followers, known as "The
Nazarenes", still manage to stir up some of the people. They
haven't caused any trouble for a long time now; but I believe
there was a disturbance shortly after his death and the
Sanhedrin took action of quite a violent nature.' He turned to
his colleague. 'Isn't that so?'

The two ministers now stood one on each side of Herod. The
Roman and the Jew. The latter, eager to have his say, welcomed
his colleague's question.

'Yes, indeed. We thought they had been completely stamped
out as a dangerous element. But it seems that those who fled
from Jerusalem after the big purge have been gathering force in
other countries. In Antioch in particular. That is where this
latest disturbance has sprung from.'

In exasperation Herod cried out:

'What disturbance? What has happened?'

At last the priest could say what he had come to say. He
spoke swiftly and with urgency:

'The Nazarenes in Antioch have collected large sums of
money and great stocks of supplies to send to the Nazarenes in
Jerusalem. All day they have been distributing food and taking
the opportunity, you may be sure, to preach of their crucified
Messiah. Some of them are outside the palace now, sharing

their bread with the people. They seem to have an unending supply.'

'What does it matter where the food comes from,' asked Agrippa, 'as long as the people are fed?'

The priest turned on him and spoke sharply.

'It matters a great deal. Already complaints have been received from the Pharisees that all this "Jesus the Messiah" hysteria is breaking out among the poor.' He faced the king again. 'The high priest himself has sent to demand that you arrest any Nazarenes who come within the precincts of the palace.'

Herod loathed to be involved in any kind of religious dispute.

'If it is a matter of religion the high priest must make his own accusations and his own arrests.'

'It is not only a matter for the high priest, sir. It is a matter that could affect your majesty most seriously. It is reported that even Gentiles are becoming members of this band of heretics. This means that the power of our Hebrew law, its codes, its punishments, may become weakened in the sight of the people. Your majesty's position depends as much upon the temple as upon the Emperor of Rome!'

Herod seemed to shrink a little into his royal Roman toga; yet he spoke defiantly.

'I am the king. Grandson of Herod the Great. My authority is in my royal blood.'

'Yet one of your majesty's own family has joined the Nazarenes in Antioch.'

'One of us, who?'

'Manaen, brother of your uncle Antipas.'

The king turned to his Roman adviser.

'What am I to do, Blastus?' The appeal sounded almost pathetic.

The chamberlain was quick to respond. He had grasped and weighed up the situation and recognized its dangers.

'It is true, your majesty, that a time of famine is a time ripe for rebellion. When people are hungry, their only loyalty is to those who feed them. And if a leader comes forward with "a new way of life", as I believe these men promise, and can at the same time feed their hungry bellies . . .' he shrugged his shoulders. 'Well, sir, I would agree that the matter is dangerous.'

Herod stood speechless between his two advisers, a majestic figure, yet a slightly ridiculous one, his face crumpled with worry and distaste at this unexpected situation, which was being thrust upon him. The sudden silence in the room made them aware that there was silence outside as well. A flicker of hope showed on Herod's troubled face. Perhaps these tiresome Nazarenes had gone. If so, there was no need for him to do anything. But it was Agrippa who went to see what was happening. The crowds had not dispersed. If anything there were more people than before. Berenice joined her brother on the balcony.

'Who are all those people lying on the ground?'

'Crippled beggars, I suppose.' replied Agrippa. 'Or starved people who are too weak to stand.'

'But they *are* standing!' Her voice was a gasp of excitement, 'Look, see that man over there.' She pointed, and the prince saw a thin, ragged figure leaning against the palace wall. 'He lies at the gates every day. Even before the famine he was there. I watch him from my window. His legs are all withered like little sticks. Look at him now, he's standing.'

Agrippa had caught her excitement. His eyes scanned the shabby crowds for some clue to this extraordinary development. Then he saw them. Two men, brothers by the look of them, who were moving quietly through the crowds. They carried no baskets of bread this time, but were laying their hands on the sick, talking to the cripples, touching the eyes of the blind. Agrippa gripped his sister's arm and spoke in a whisper:

'Look, it's those two over there. . . Keep very quiet and we'll hear what they're saying.'

Berenice held her breath. Very faintly from below the voices reached them.

'In the name of Jesus the Messiah, stand up and walk . . . I have no more bread to give you, but receive your sight. . . I believe in Jesus the Messiah. . . Your faith has made you whole. . . Praise to the Lord Jesus, who gives life. . .'

The prince turned and called to his father:

'They're making lame men walk and blind men see! Who are those men?'

Herod and his two ministers crossed quickly to stand beside the children. They listened for a moment while the voices floated up to them. Then the priest spoke in great agitation:

'This must be stopped. We had this very thing in the temple just before the high priest ordered the purge. This feeding and healing of the poor is more dangerous than all their words of blasphemy.'

'Since when was it a crime to heal the sick?' asked the young prince sternly.

'What is it, witchcraft?' said the princess, awed and excited.

The king spoke more to himself than to the others:

'Miracle workers! Miracle workers at my very gates,' he muttered.

The priest continued as though no one had spoken:

'If you allow it to go on, your majesty, the thing will grow out of all control. Then the civil court will intervene and you will find yourself robbed of all power. You must show the people now that a Herod can once more be called "The Great".'

'Herod the Great,' murmured the king. He was wavering. Agrippa looked at him, amazed and shocked.

'But he was a tyrant, father!'

To do right in his son's eyes was more important to Herod than anything in the world. He drew himself up and echoed the words, albeit rather half-heartedly:

'My grandfather was a tyrant.'

The priest knew how to appeal to the king's vanity and dreams of glory. He was not going to allow a stripling prince to undermine his influence. His voice rose:

'Your grandfather put thousands of innocent children to the sword when it was only whispered that a new king of Israel had been born. Your uncle executed the man who heralded the approach of one "Greater than kings". But you. . .' He let scorn colour the words, 'you see your nation riddled with traitors, have this false Messiah's name hurled against you at your palace gates, and will not lift a finger to save your kingdom.'

Clearly the king was shaken. Once more he appealed to his Roman adviser.

'Blastus?'

The chamberlain's approach was different. Practical, urbane, unemotional.

'I think that the attitude of Rome would be that sedition of any kind, wherever or in whatever unusual form it should be found, must be stamped out. Nipped in the bud.'

'By force?'

'By force if necessary.'

Against his will, Agrippa found himself influenced by the official Roman attitude. But made one last appeal:

'But there may be hundreds of them. My father isn't a tyrant. He doesn't massacre his own countrymen.'

'Bloodshed may not be necessary, if action is taken quickly,' continued Blastus, quietly taking command of the situation. 'Arrest those two down there, get from them the name of their present leader, and find out where their headquarters are.'

'Supposing they won't tell?' interjected Berenice, pleasurably frightened by the turn of events. 'Will they be tortured?'

Herod reasserted himself. Wasn't he king? The priest was right, he too would be known as 'The Great'.

'A man who will not speak when his king commands will be put to the sword.' He threw out his arm in a majestic gesture. 'Go, Blastus.'

The chamberlain hurried out. Berenice gave a little gasp of morbid anticipation, but Agrippa, greatly troubled, caught hold of the outstretched hand.

'Father!'

Swiftly the priest intervened.

'You have acted wisely, sir. In the words of the high priest on another occasion, "It is better that one man should die for the people than that a whole nation should perish".'

In the upstairs room Rhoda was putting out plates and cups.
'Though the Lord alone knows,' she thought, 'whether there'll
be anything to go on them.' They'd told her to prepare for
supper every night as usual ever since the famine had begun.
But many nights there had been nothing to eat. And now, when
all this food and money had come from Antioch, instead of
stocking up the larder they'd taken the whole lot out with them
this morning, money and food as well. 'Oh, well,' she thought,
'I suppose they know best.' And she hummed a little song to
herself as she worked, to help her forget how hungry she was.

The door opened and Peter came into the room carrying a
large basket in his arms. Rhoda smiled up at him eagerly as he
set the basket down and reached into it.

'There you are, Rhoda, that's for our supper,' he said, putting into her hands a few small loaves of bread.

'Well,' said Rhoda, 'you haven't left much for yourselves, I
must say.' She counted the loaves out on to the table: 'Five little
bits of bread between you lot, and goodness knows how many
poor souls they'll bring back with them.'

Peter smiled. As if to himself he said, 'Five loaves and two
fish.'

'Where's the fish?'

He seemed to come out of a dream. 'Not even any fish today.
But do you know, Rhoda, once when we were with the master,
5,000 people had gathered to hear him speak. Camped all over
the hills, they were, and there they stayed until dark. Miles from
any village. We thought they'd begin to get restless when they
got hungry, because they didn't seem to have brought any food
with them.'

'Knowing you, I don't suppose you had any for yourselves
either,' scolded Rhoda.

'We had five loaves and two small fish.'

'I know what you're going to tell me,' she sighed. 'You went
and gave them all away.'

'Yes. That's just what we did do. We shared what we had with all those people.'

'With 5,000?' Rhoda laughed. 'There must have been a lot went hungry.'

'No. Not one. Every man, woman and child in that huge crowd was fed and satisfied. What's more, we collected twelve baskets, baskets as big as this one here, full of scraps when they'd had enough.'

Rhoda was used to miracles, but this beat them all. She just gasped.

'That was the day,' continued Peter, 'when the people shouted out, "Jesus the king".'

'I don't wonder!' gasped Rhoda.

Peter sat down and began to undo his sandals.

'I've been thinking all day about that,' he said. 'Going round feeding the people with all this food from Antioch, wondering if there'd be enough to go round... I've remembered that day.'

Suddenly footsteps were heard running up the stairs. The door burst open and John staggered in. He was dishevelled and out of breath. He slammed the door, then leaned against it gasping. Peter sprang up and went over to him.

'John, what is it? What's happened? Where is James?'

'He's been arrested.'

Rhoda stifled a scream and, with shaking hands, managed to pour a cup of water. Peter held it to John's lips. He gulped it down and then gasped out his story.

'We were outside Herod's palace, giving food to the people who'd gathered there... It was the king's guards... They came out suddenly and drove the crowds away... Then they seized hold of us and asked the name of our leader and where our meeting place was. James protested that they had no right to arrest us... We were in a public street and had done nothing against the law... Suddenly they all drew their swords... That's when I managed to break free, but they held James... I think they took him into the palace... I ran as fast as I could to warn you ... but they may have followed... You must get away, Peter, and somehow we must warn the others.'

But it was too late. Feet clattered through the yard and up the stairs. The three in the room, realizing they were trapped, turned to face the door. It burst open and two of Herod's soldiers stood framed in the doorway.

'There he is,' shouted one, pointing at John. His companion seized John. Rhoda tried to slip out of the door and was herself seized.

In the words of his master Peter called out:

'I am the man you are looking for, let these others go free.'

They looked at him.

'You are the leader?'

'Yes.'

The soldiers grinned. Here was a prize indeed. They released John and Rhoda and took hold of Peter, chaining his arms behind him. As they hustled him towards the door John stepped in front of them.

'Where is my brother?'

The soldiers looked at each other. Then one of them said:

'Your brother, was it? He's down below.' He strolled to the door and shouted down the stairs, 'Bring him up.'

Feet stumbled up the narrow stairs and then in the doorway stood two more soldiers carrying between them the body of James. Without a word they dropped their burden at John's feet, then dragged their prisoner from the room. John and Rhoda stood frozen with shock as the feet clattered down the stairs and across the yard. Then Rhoda covered her face and sank on to the floor weeping quietly. John knelt down beside his dead brother. He too was weeping. Then, as he cradled the head in his arms and looked down on the well-loved face, he remembered one of the last things Jesus had said to them in this room. Rhoda raised her head as she heard him whisper:

'The greatest love a person can have for his friends is to give his life for them.'

Simon Peter lay asleep in his prison cell. Beside him on the ground sat two guards to whom his wrists were chained. They too were sleeping. The heavy door was barred on the outside and sixteen soldiers had been put by Herod on special duty to guard the prisoner's cell.

In his sleep, Peter became aware of a light shining on his face, and a voice saying: 'Quick, get up.' He opened his eyes and saw a man standing in front of him. Peter rubbed his eyes, wondering if he was awake or dreaming. The man spoke again. 'Get up and put on your sandals.' Peter looked at his hands. To his amazement he saw that the chains had fallen from his wrists and that he was free. Quickly he slipped his feet into his sandals and stood up. 'Now put on your coat and follow me.' Still thinking that he was dreaming, he followed the man out of the open door of the cell, past the soldiers in the corridor, right up to the great iron gate that led into the street. The gate swung open and Peter and his companion stepped out into the silent, moonlit city.

In the upstairs room all was quiet as the brethren of the city prayed for their leader, who had so suddenly been snatched away from them.

Rhoda was the first to hear a sudden sharp knock on the gate of the courtyard. Startled, she raised her head and looked round the silent gathering. Nobody else seemed to have heard it. Her legs trembled and her heart beat with fear as she got to her feet. It was part of her duties to open the gate. She knew she should go and not disturb the others, but suppose it was the soldiers again? Nobody noticed her as she slipped out of the room. She ran down the stairs and across the dark, deserted courtyard, then stood by the locked gate, listening.

At the second loud, urgent knock her heart nearly stopped beating. For a moment she could not speak, and then in a trembling little voice she asked timidly:

'Who is it?'

'It is I, Peter, open the door.'

At the sound of the familiar voice, which she never expected to hear again, Rhoda lost her head completely. Laughing and crying she called out:

'Peter? Oh, oh, oh, God be praised, sir, you're free. God be praised, he has heard our prayers,' and in her excitement completely forgetting to open the gate she ran up the stairs shouting, 'Masters, masters, Peter's come home. Peter's come home!' The knocking on the gate continued as she burst into the upstairs room: 'It's Peter. There at the gate.' One by one the brethren rose to their feet, staring at her in astonishment.

'You're mad, girl,' said James the Just.

'It is! It is!' cried Rhoda. 'I'd know his voice anywhere.'

'Perhaps it's his spirit,' whispered Mark.

The knocking continued, loud and urgent. Rhoda turned and dashed down the stairs again, followed by Mark and Barnabas. Rhoda would have unbarred the gate at once, but Barnabas stopped her and called:

'Who's there?'

'Is that you, Barnabas? For the love of God, open the door.'

As Rhoda had said, there was no mistaking that voice. Quickly Barnabas unbarred the gate and pulled Peter inside. The two men embraced him warmly, while Rhoda, her voice rising to a joyful shout, danced round them:

'There, you see! I'm sorry, sir, I was so excited I forgot to open the door.'

'Ssh!' said Peter. 'Not so loud.'

'Come upstairs quickly,' urged Barnabas, but Peter shook his head.

'No, I won't come in. This is the first place they'd look for me.'

'How did you get out?' whispered Mark.

'Someome let me out.'

'Who?'

'I thought at first I was dreaming. He came right into the cell where I was sleeping . . . I followed him out into the street and then, he disappeared.'

'An angel?' asked Rhoda, in an awed whisper.

'I don't know. But whether it was a man or an angel, it was the Lord's doing.'

For a moment none of them could speak because their joy and thankfulness was so great. Then Barnabas remembered the present emergency.

'Where will you go now, Peter?'

'The Lord will show me, don't be afraid. But this may mean the end of our church in Jerusalem, for a while, anyway, so I'll tell you what you must do. Go to Tarsus, Barnabas, and find our brother, Saul. Take him with you to Antioch. You remember what he said about being a witness to the Gentiles? Well, tell him his time has come. You and he together strengthen the church in Antioch. Take young Mark with you. Now tell the other brethren up there what I have told you, and the Lord be with you all.'

Then Peter embraced his friends, placed his hands for a moment on Rhoda's head, and slipped away into the night.

5
From
Saul to Paul

ANTIOCH of Syria was the greatest and richest city of the east, the third greatest city in the Roman Empire, ranking next in importance to Rome and Alexandria. The colonnaded streets were paved with marble. There were racecourses, theatres, baths, fountains and temples to every god under the sun in this sophisticated cosmopolitan city where the culture of Greece, the civilization of Rome, the mystery and wisdom of the east were mingled.

In the market places Roman officials, Greek artists, Jewish merchants, jugglers, beggars, dancers, townsmen in their long silk robes, peasants from the nearby villages in their short rough tunics and high leather boots, freemen and slaves of every race and colour went about their business or stood and gossiped.

Two young men, students by the look of them, were having an animated conversation as they walked through this busy, lively throng. Suddenly one of them stopped, catching his companion by the arm.

'Look,' he said. 'See that big black fellow. He was at the university with me.'

His friend saw a tall, strong-looking African standing with a group of men on the other side of the street.

'Symeon Niger he's called. By Zeus he's changed.'

'In what way?'

'Well he used to be such a serious, heavy fellow. A great student of Hebrew religion and law, always reading and fasting and imitating the Jews—' The young man broke off in embarrassment, then turned to his friend with a laugh. '—Sorry, Silas, but you know how it is with the converts to your faith. They become more Jewish than the Jews.' The young Jew smiled. 'Anyway, poor old Symeon used to look as though he carried all the troubles of the world on his shoulders. Well, look at him now.'

They looked across the street again. The African was laughing with his friends, and many of the passers-by turned to look at the extraordinarily happy bunch of men.

'I can tell you something about them.' His friend's tone was so serious that Titus looked at him in surprise.

'You can?'

'Yes. They're a new sect. It started in the synagogue. They worship "The Christ".'

'What's that? A new god? Wonders will never cease if the Jews have found a new god!' Then, as his freind made no comment, he asked: 'What do they call themselves, this sect?'

'The brotherhood.'

Titus found his curiosity mounting. 'And what does this new god, this—Christ—do for them?' he asked.

'I don't know. But they're a happy lot. I've heard it said that they've discovered new ways of healing the sick. I don't suppose there's anything in that. But they do a lot of good among the poor.'

'Healing the sick, eh? I must say that interests me. Let's go and talk to them.'

Titus was just about to cross the street when Silas held him by the shoulder.

'Wait a moment, there's three more joined them. Travellers by the look of them.'

Symeon welcomed his friend Barnabas with a joyful shout. The other travellers, a tent-maker carrying his tools, and a young man who seemed to be the sort of secretary of the party, for he carried scrolls and brushes, he had not met before. Barnabas introduced them as Saul of Tarsus and John Mark of Jerusalem. Symeon embraced the strangers warmly and presented them to his fellow leaders of the brotherhood in Antioch, Lucius of Cyrene and Manaen of the Herodians. Saul's eyes burned with an eager excitement. He seemed like a man who had returned home after a long exile. Only young Mark stood a little aloof; startled and confused by the strange non-Hebrew atmosphere of the city and of these fellow brethren.

After the greetings Symeon turned his beaming smile on his friend:

'What's the news from Jerusalem, Barnabas?'

'Bad news, I'm afraid.' Symeon's smile faded. 'But have courage, brother, there's a great deal of work to be done here. Where can we go to talk?'

'Come to my lodgings,' said the African, putting an arm round his friend's shoulder and leading him off down the street.

'Symeon?'

Symeon turned and saw a young man racing towards him. His face lit up in recognition and he held out his arms.

'Titus!' The young man ran up to him. 'It's good to see you. How are you, boy?'

'I'm well,' panted Titus, 'and so are you by the looks of you. Tell me, is it true that you serve a strange new god?'

'*What!*' The African roared with laughter. 'You know me better than that. I leave strange gods to you men of Greece and Rome!'

'I heard you were a . . . a . . . "Christ man".'

'"Christ man"? Its the first time I've heard that name!' laughed Symeon, and then seeing the look of inquiry in the other's eyes, which belied the mockery of his tone, he spoke more seriously:

'But I know what you refer to. Do you want to know more

about the Christ we serve?'

'Yes. I do.'

'Then come to one of our meetings.'

'Where?'

'At my lodings, the same old ones in Signon Street.'

'When?'

Symeon smiled delightedly at the young man's impatience.

'Any evening. You'll be very welcome.'

'You can expect me.'

Symeon led his guests down the street towards his lodgings. Silas joined Titus where he stood looking after them.

'What did he say?'

'He's invited me to one of his meetings. I'm going.'

Silas laughed. It was his turn to tease his friend.

'You'll become a Christ man yet, Titus. You'll have to mend your ways if you do.'

'Why?'

'Well, for all their gaiety, I hear they're against a lot of things that go on in this city. Don't forget it's a Jewish sect.'

Titus grinned at him. 'We have our religion too, you know.'

'Maybe,' said Silas, determined to have the last word. 'But it's often in the name of religion that the worst crimes are committed.'

'You're as bad as my tutor,' laughed Titus. 'He was saying that only the other day—"Religion in this city, nowadays . . .",' he imitated an old man's voice, '". . . consists of corrupting oneself with a thousand crimes and in stripping oneself of the last traces of virtue".'

Silas laughed while Titus continued in his normal voice.

'You'd better come too, Silas, and keep your stern Hebrew eye on me. Who knows, perhaps we'll both become "Christ men".'

Titus and Silas were only two of the thousands of Jews and Gentiles who joined the brotherhood of Christ in Antioch. The name 'Christ men', became widely adopted and very soon was abbreviated, so that the brethren of Antioch were known to those outside the church as 'Christians'.

Saul worked hard at his trade of tent-making, and while he worked at his loom or with needles and thread, he talked to those who came to the lodgings, customers, peasants, scholars, beggars, merchants, students, travellers—he talked to them non-stop about the love of God, the brotherhood of man, and the new life that had been given to them through the risen Christ. Day after day, after his work, he preached in the streets and market places, and each day he brought new believers into the brotherhood by his enthusiasm and his gift of words.

To Barnabas it was a never-ending source of wonder and joy to see the same fervour and religious zeal that had inflamed Saul the persecutor, now burning in Saul the apostle of Christ. He wished they could travel even farther afield, 'Into every part of the world' as the Lord had told them, and let that flame of faith and love be a torch to bring light to people everywhere. He prayed that this chance might come. His prayer was answered and one day he, Saul and Mark, said farewell to the 'Christians' of Antioch and went down to the harbour of Seleucia to set sail for Cyprus.

Paphos on the north-west coast of Cyprus was the seat of the island's Roman governor. His villa stood next to the beautiful temple of Venus amid the orange and lemon trees that grew in abundance in this part of the island. Sergius Paulus was an intelligent man and, like so many of his countrymen whose duties took them to the east, he found himself dissatisfied with the gods of his fathers and deeply interested in the religion of the Jews.

Today he sat on his terrace, listening with impatience to the chanting of a professional sorcerer who claimed to have divine powers and the gift of prophecy. He watched this man drawing the signs of the zodiac in the sand, then challenged him irritably:

'Well, what new thing have you to tell me, Elymas?'

The sorcerer stopped his chanting and in a high sing-song voice proclaimed his 'prophecies':

'Most worthy Proconsul, under the sign of Venus, you will be loved. In the name of Artemis, your wife will be fruitful, by the sign of Mars, you will conquer your enemies . . .'

Sergius interrupted him brusquely. 'I have heard all this before, and what does it mean? In the name of Venus and Artemis and Mars? What magic is there in these names? Have you no new marvels to show me?'

'Any marvel under the sun that my master desires.'

Sergius leaned forward and stared into the man's face:

'Can you heal the sick? Can you cast out devils? Can you raise the dead? No, you cannot. But there are those who can.' He called to his servant: 'Are those three Jews here yet?'

'They are waiting, sir.'

'Bring them in.' The servant withdrew. 'Now you may see and hear some new wonders, Elymas.'

'No wonder that is not known to me, sir,' protested the sorcerer. 'I have studied the secrets of the stars. I have looked into the future and into the past. I know the ways of the Most High God.' But Sergius Paulus was not listening. He had risen to greet three travel-stained strangers who were ushered with some ceremony on to the terrace. The proconsul held out his hand to the tallest of the three who seemed to be their leader.

'What is your name?'

'Joseph Barnabas, sir, a native of this island.' He turned to introduce the others: 'My nephew, John Mark of Jerusalem, and my friend Saul of Tarsus.'

To Mark's surprise, Saul stepped forward to address the proconsul himself. He was further surprised by his words.

'Of Tarsus, but a Roman citizen, sir.'

Sergius looked at him with interest. 'Indeed, how is that?'

'My family are tent-makers, sir. My father was given Roman citizenship as a reward for his work in the Roman army.'

'I see.' The proconsul held out his hand, and as Saul gripped his forearm in the Roman fashion, said with a laugh, 'Not Saul, but *Paul* of Tarsus, eh?' Mark felt a twinge of annoyance as the proconsul invited 'Paul' to sit by him while Barnabas remained standing. He glanced at his uncle, but neither surprise nor jealousy showed on his face.

Sergius Paulus was speaking.

'Tell me,' he said, 'what new teaching is this that you have brought to the Jews in Cyprus? There is a new life among them, a new spirit. Do you still worship the same God?'

'The one true God.'

'One true God,' echoed Sergius. 'I wish I could believe that.'

Immediately Elymas thrust himself between them. 'One God all powerful indeed. One God writes in the stars for his chosen prophets to read, who gives his chosen servants the gift of prophecy, who endows his prophets with mysterious powers to call on the names of his holy ones to perform miracles. . .'

'You are wrong.' It was the stranger, 'Paul', who interrupted him. 'There is only one name under heaven. The name of Jesus, the Christ.'

'The Christ?' repeated Sergius, perplexed. 'What does that mean?'

With a scream the sorcerer pointed an accusing finger at Paul.

'This Jew is a blasphemer. He would make a man into a god.'

Nobody paid any attention. Paul spoke quietly to his host.

'The Christ is the Messiah. The Holy One chosen by God. It is through him that this new, this Holy Spirit has come into the world.'

'Where is he?'

'Yes, where is he?' Elymas sidled up to Paul. 'Can you show him to us? Is he man or spirit? And if spirit, is he good or evil? Show the proconsul your tricks, Paul of Tarsus, call up your Christ. Conjure him up before us if you can.'

Again Paul ignored him. 'You said, sir, that you wished you could believe the one all powerful God. Christ is the visible expression of the one all powerful God through whom everything was made, spiritual and material, seen and unseen. You are a man who holds authority. Understand, then, that it was through him and for him, the Lord and Creator of life, that power and ownership and authority were created.'

'Through him or through the emperor?'

'The emperor is a servant of the living God. He who created

us and the world in which we live, to him must belong the power and the glory.'

'Fool!' The sorcerer was standing right behind Paul and hissed the word in his ear. 'How can you dare to talk like this before the proconsul? Are you so ignorant that you do not know that it is the law of Rome to worship the emperor.' His voice rose into a scream again. 'You call yourself a Roman citizen, yet you dare insult the emperor to his own officer?'

'Be silent!'

He cringed away like a dog at the harsh tone of his master who was looking at Paul with a growing interest.

'You have not answered my question. I asked you where is this Christ whom you call the visible expression of your invisible God?'

'He lives in us, his messengers.'

Sergius frowned. 'I don't understand that.'

The whipped dog crawled back to its master's feet. 'If your most gracious excellency will allow me to speak, I would question this . . . renegade Roman . . . this blasphemous Jew, who so cunningly evades your excellency's questions.'

'Very well.'

Elymas smiled and took his place beside the proconsul. He addressed his rival smoothly, like a lawyer in a court of law who hopes to trap a witness.

'Will you tell his excellency what happened under Roman law to this Jesus whom you call Christ?'

Paul did not hesitate. 'He was crucified.'

'Crucified!' The Roman's disappointment was tinged with distaste. 'You mean he was just an ordinary man who died . . . who died a criminal's death? . . . What makes you think that such a person could be your God become man?'

'Because he rose from the dead.'

The proconsul leaned forward and stared at the man who made this amazing statement. The dark eyes were calm and matched the certainty of the words he had spoken. His interest quickened. 'You mean he came to life again?'

'Then where is he?' The sorcerer's voice cut across the moment like a lash. 'For the third time, where is he? Show us the man who died and rose to life again and now speaks through the mouth of Saul, the tent-maker. Tell his excellency what he should do that your crucified Christ will reveal himself in his "power and glory".'

For the first time, Paul looked at Elymas. Then he answered with the same quiet simplicity.

'He will reveal himself to every man that believes. Three things only are needed. Faith and hope and love.'

With a scornful, triumphant laugh Elymas turned to his master, but Paul was before him, and now his words poured out.

'Your excellency, I am not ashamed of the truth I preach, for it is the very power of God working for the salvation of everyone who believes it—Jew, or Greek, or Roman. All who follow the leading of God's spirit are members of the very family of God. For he created us in his image and then sent to us his own Son to be the eldest of a family of many brothers; and we are not meant to remain as children, at the mercy of every chance wind of teaching, or of men who are expert in the crafty presentation of lies, but we are meant to hold firmly to the truth, and to grow up in every way.'

'The truth,' echoed Sergius. 'If we knew the truth. . .'

It was the question that troubled the hearts of men everywhere. The question to which Paul himself knew only part of the answer. But what he did know he would give.

'The truth we do know is that there is one God, the Father of us all; and one Spirit working through us and living in us all. At present we only understand a fraction of what it means. We are like men who see the hazy reflection of a landscape in a glass; but the time will come when we shall see the truth face to face, and whole, and understand it as fully as God now understands us.'

Sergius Paulus sat silent for a moment. When he spoke it was almost to himself.

'Faith and hope and love? It sounds so simple and it feels like the truth. Yet, if true and if we lived by it, it could change the whole world.'

Elymas was greatly disturbed to see the impression that Paul had made on the proconsul. He determined to break the spell.

'Faith in what? A dead man? Hope for what? Rewards from heaven? And love! ... Love for whom? For thieves and murderers? ... Your excellency, this man has bewitched you with meaningless words. You are a man of wisdom and learning. By his own admission this false prophet has no use for such things. . .' He gave a clever imitation of Paul's voice. '"All I know is a little fraction of the truth".' Then he moved forward and spat his bitter mocking words right into Paul's face. 'Why don't you study to learn the whole truth? Why did your all powerful God give us brains and sensitivity and powers if all he demands is "faith and hope and love"?'

Paul's eyes blazed. He stood up and, though a small man, he seemed to tower over the other. 'You son of the devil. You enemy of all good. You *know* that I speak the truth.' Elymas shrank before the sudden authority of his rival's tone. He would have retreated, but the eyes which seemed to burn into his own held him transfixed while the voice continued. 'Well, I know how the Lord deals with those who try to twist the straight path that leads to him. As long as you try to blind others to the goodness of God, you yourself will be blind and live in darkness until you see the light of truth.'

With a cry, Elymas covered his eyes with his hands. Sergius leapt to his feet. Barnabas and Mark stood dumb with amazement as the sorcerer began to whimper: 'Help me, lead me. . .' He stretched out his hands to them, groping in the air.'Take my hand . . . lead me . . .' Nobody moved. The proconsul stared at Paul with a new awe.

'You have the power to strike men blind?'

'No,' said Paul. 'I don't, but God does. Once I too tried to divert men from the truth and I, too, was struck blind. For it is a sin against life itself to put obstacles in the way of those who are looking for the truth.'

The awe and wonder were still in his voice as Sergius Paulus spoke the words that Paul had longed to hear.

'I believe it is the truth.'

On the deck of the small boat that carried them away from Cyprus Barnabas stood watching the shores of his homeland recede into the distance.

'Did you want to leave Cyprus so soon?' The speaker was Mark who stood beside his uncle, a worried frown on his face.

'Paul thought that we had finished our work there.'

Mark was irritated. 'Why does he call himself Paul now?'

'He's a Roman citizen, and it's his name as much as Saul is. Outside Jerusalem it's as well to have a name that isn't only Hebrew.'

Mark sighed. 'I don't think I'll ever get used to it.'

Barnabas turned to look at him in surprise.

'What?'

'Mixing with Romans and Greeks and talking to them about our scriptures.'

Barnabas saw the young mouth tremble and was just about to say some words of comfort when a voice rang out: 'Barnabas!' They turned to see Paul striding towards them. His hair blowing in the wind, his bare feet sure on the rolling deck, he looked to Mark more like a sailor than a tent-maker, and when he spoke he might have been the captain of the ship. 'I have decided the route we should take. This ship will land us at Attalia. There's a community of brethren there. We'll go on to Perga, work our way through Asia to Ephesus and then to Troy.' He was exhilarated, impetuous and in complete command. 'Well, what do you say to that?'

Mark's heart sank. 'When will we be back in Jerusalem?'

'Who knows? Perhaps not until we have been to Rome.'

'Rome?'

Paul threw back his head and laughed.

'Some day I mean to go to Rome.'

Mark could bear it no longer. Without a word he turned and walked away. Paul looked after him. 'What's the matter with Mark? Is he ill?'

'No,' said Barnabas. 'Perhaps a little homesick.'

Paul frowned. 'He asked to come with us. Surely he knew that we must go where the Spirit leads us. Is he a man or a child?'

'He's only a boy still. Give him time.'

Mark leaned against the ship's side, gazing with unseeing eyes at the blue water. Longing for his homeland, resentment at Paul's sudden assumption of leadership, shame at his own inability to keep up with his two companions, dragged his spirits down to near despair. Lost in his own thoughts he didn't know that Barnabas had come to find him until he felt a hand on his shoulder. He knew who it was without looking round. Still staring down at the sea he said: 'It's no good. I can't go on.'

'We need you, Mark.'

'Do you?' His voice was flat and unbelieving.

'What's the trouble? Things moving too fast for you?'

'Too fast and too far.'

'There's no place too far. "Go to all the nations of the earth." That's what the Lord said.'

Mark made no reply. Barnabas leant over the side with him and went on talking. 'Everywhere there are men, there are children of God. How are they to learn the truth unless we take it to them?'

'But how do we know that this is the right time?'

The thoughts that had been tormenting Mark for days now came pouring out. 'How do we know that they're ready for it? Our ancestors lived in darkness for centuries before God revealed himself to them; and then there was generation after generation of prophets and teachers ... thousands of years of faith in God before the Messiah came with his message of forgiveness and hope. ... How can we expect these heathens who have nothing behind them but generations of idol-worship and superstition, who turn from one god to another as easily as they change their clothes, to be suddenly converted into God-fearing men because Saul comes to them with his gospel of faith and hope and love?'

'We aren't alone, Mark.'

'I know.' For a moment shame overwhelmed the other

emotions and he buried his head in his hands. 'I haven't forgotten him, Barnabas. I swear to you that I haven't lost my faith.' Then he raised his head and looked earnestly into his uncle's face. 'But we can make mistakes. . . You see, Saul and you never saw Jesus, when he was with us in the flesh. I did. I was only a child when he came to our house, but I remember him and the things he said. Things so vivid they'd stay in a child's mind. . . "Don't throw your pearls in front of pigs," he said, "or the pigs may trample on them and then turn to gore you" . . . I laughed at the time, imagining a lot of pigs knee-deep in pearls. But I've thought of that a lot since . . . I thought of it yesterday in that Roman court.'

Barnabas thought for a moment and then said with a smile: 'But the "pig" didn't turn to gore us. He believed.'

'For a moment, yes. But for how long?' The anxious questions tumbled out. 'Shouldn't we have stayed in Cyprus? You and me anyway? Shouldn't we have built up a church of believers there the same way as in Antioch? Are they really better off than before we went?'

'Yes. They are. The yeast is in the bread.'

'What?'

'When your mother makes bread she puts the yeast inside and leaves the bread to rise. She doesn't stay and watch and worry that it won't do its job. She trusts the living yeast. . . That's another of the master's stories. Peter told it me.'

Mark put his head in his hands again. His voice betrayed his inner conflict as he asked in hardly more than a whisper: 'Have I failed you?'

'No.' Barnabas put his hand on the young man's shoulder. 'It's like Paul said. We're all members of the same body, and we each have our special job to do. Hands serve the body one way, feet another. Eyes and ears, tongue and teeth have different functions but belong to the same head. Christ is our head and we do our work in him. It would be stupid for any one member to think that another had failed because it had been designed to do a different job.'

'I thought this was my job.'

'It may be yet. But perhaps you're not quite ready. Like feet that can walk but haven't yet learned to run!'

Mark looked up. 'If I leave you . . . if I go back . . . will Paul be angry?'

Not for a moment did Barnabas betray his suspicion that Paul would indeed be very angry. 'I'll speak to him,' he said with a reassuring smile and went off to find him, leaving Mark still deep in thought.

The three missionaries travelled together as far as Perga in Pamphylia, and there Mark left the others to continue the journey alone. It was an unhappy parting, for even Barnabas couldn't persuade Paul to think of Mark but as a deserter. As Mark watched them plodding away up the rugged mountain path, he was torn between the desire to run after them and the longing for his own people which tugged at his heart. He watched until they were out of sight and then began his lonely journey back to Jerusalem.

Paul and Barnabas travelled through the countries of Galatia and Pisidia, preaching in the synagogues that Jesus who was crucified was Israel's Messiah. It was a hard journey, for the towns and villages lay many miles apart and the roads between were often only mountain tracks. Paul's health began to fail him, but though his body was often racked with pain and his face showed the marks of his suffering, he seemed to be driven on by an inner strength, by something that burned within him and could not be quenched.

These were pagan countries, some of them Roman garrison towns, others cities in which the Greek influence predominated, and some smaller towns and villages where the inhabitants seemed to have escaped either influence and worshipped even older gods. But in each place there was a Jewish community, and where there were Jews there was a synagogue, and it was in the synagogues that Paul and Barnabas delivered their message. When Paul preached, the sick and weary traveller was transformed. It was as though the flame of life itself, life as God gave it to man uncorrupted, joyous, filled with grace and truth, burned in him like a torch and poured from his lips in words of fire.

But the rulers in these remote synagogues were by no means happy to see their members flocking to these travelling preachers who brought such a strange and disturbing message. In Iconium the small Jewish community had added to its number proselytes from among some of the richest and most influential Gentile citizens, and on the sabbath day that Paul and Barnabas were invited to speak the synagogue was crowded. After the chief rabbi had read from the Law and the prophets, he addressed the two visitors. 'My brothers, we welcome you to our synagogue. If you have any message of encouragement for the people we will be glad to hear you speak.'

Paul rose and took his place beside the rabbi. 'Men of Israel, and all you who honour God.' His voice rang out, reaching not only those inside the synagogue, but the crowd of pagans who had gathered round the open door. 'The message that we bring to you is this: the promise that was made to our ancestors has been fulfilled. 'The Holy One of Israel', God's own dear Son, born as God promised from the line of David, the long-awaited Messiah has come to us.'

There was a rustle and a murmuring among the people and the rabbi sat forward in his chair, startled. The speaker continued. 'He did not come unannounced. You remember God's promise, "I will send my messenger ahead of you to open the way for you." That messenger was a man of our own time called John who spent his life urging the people of Israel to prepare themselves for their Messiah and baptizing them in the name of the one who was about to come. So the people of Israel were prepared for their Messiah. . . . And he came to them even while John was still preparing them.'

The rabbi sat tense as excited whispers and rumours of disbelief broke out in his congregation.

'Yes, my friends.' They grew quiet again, watching the speaker. 'After John, God sent his own Son to live among his people as a man among men. . . But the people of Jerusalem and their rulers would not recognize him. Will you believe it when I tell you that they arrested their Messiah and persuaded the governor to have him executed as a criminal?'

Again the voices broke out and now there were gasps of horror mingled with the excitement and disbelief.

'But we see now that even this was what the scriptures said would happen. You remember the words: "He is despised and rejected of men. . . Like a lamb about to be slaughtered . . ."? Jesus the Saviour was crucified; but that wasn't the end. It was in a way the beginning. There was another prophecy to come true: "God will not abandon his Holy One to the world of the dead" . . . Jesus died on the cross, his body was buried in a tomb, but . . . God raised him from the dead.'

There was no murmuring now, but to the rabbi the silence that followed these astounding words was more ominous. Like the silence before an earthquake. His senses and his active scholar's brain seemed to be at war within him as he waited with the others for what might follow. As if in answer to an unspoken question Paul's voice rose again: 'He was seen by those who had come from Galilee with him, men who had worked with him for three years and were at the foot of the cross when he died. They talked and ate with him for many days after he had risen from the dead. These men are his witnesses in Jerusalem. We are his witnesses to you. We come to tell you the good news. . . Forgiveness of your sins is offered to you through this man Jesus, even those sins from which the law of Moses could never set you free. Only one thing is necessary, that you believe in him.'

The silence of the rapt congregation was disturbed as with angry mutters several of the older men began to push their way through to the door. Paul saw them and called out: 'Be careful, my brothers, that the prophet's reprimand does not apply to you.' The men paused and half turned to face him, embarrassed at being singled out in this way but unwilling to appear churlish. Paul unrolled the scroll in his hand and quietly read the prophet's words. '"Look upon this, you scornful souls, and lose yourselves in astonishment. Such wonders I am doing in your days, that if a man told you the story you would not believe it".' The well-known words that had been read in that synagogue on so many sabbath days seemed suddenly to spring to life. It seemed to the rabbi that he was hearing them for the first time. And as Paul rolled up the scroll and descended from the speaker's platform, he rose as though he was about to speak to him, but no words came. Paul bowed to him and then strode through the silent crowds, past the hostile men who stood staring at him with cold astonishment and, joining Barnabas, stepped out into the sunlight.

Immediately the two missionaries were surrounded by the pagan citizens who had been listening from the door, and the women from the upper gallery who had raced down the steps to greet them. The congregation poured through the doors to join the crowd outside, and their loud excited voices reached the rabbi as he stood alone in the empty synagogue.

What was he to think? What was he to do? All his years of work, the faith of his ancestors, the Hebrew law, that he had so strictly observed and taught, all seemed to be crashing about his ears. Life had not been easy for him in this remote pagan district, so far from the homeland. It had not been easy to guard and guide his flock. But he had succeeded not only in this, but had managed to win converts to the Jewish faith from among some of the most influential citizens. Gentile men and women who gave generously to support the synagogue and the poorer Jews. But what now? Already his flock seemed to have deserted him to follow the bearer of some fantastic news. Israel's Messiah had come. Was it fantastic? Could it conceivably be true? What would his rich proselytes think? What did the authorities in Jerusalem say? Who could advise him? He was not left alone for long.

'Rabbi! Rabbi!'

A rich merchant, one of the most influential Jews in the town, bustled up to him.

'What does it mean, rabbi? What are you going to do?'

Still dazed, the rabbi answered, 'I don't know.'

'Did you know they were going to speak like that?'

The rabbi came out of his reverie for a moment. Here was a

question he could answer.

'No. How could I know? They were visitors from the homeland. Men of our faith straight from Jerusalem. Naturally I asked them to address us, to give us any message from the land of Israel. How could I have guessed that their message would be . . . this?'

Before the merchant could speak, another man had joined them, scarcely more than a boy. 'Rabbi. Is it true what these men say? That the Messiah has come?'

Here was the question he could not answer. He looked at the boy's flushed, excited face. 'I don't know.'

The merchant was shocked. '*Don't know?* You must know.' He stared at the clouded eyes, the dazed expression. 'Rabbi! You don't mean that *you* believe that this fantastic story could be true?'

'Rabbi, is it true?' They stood one on each side of him, the representatives of his flock, old and orthodox, young and wondering. And he, the shepherd, could not lead them. 'Hundreds of our people are following these men to their lodgings. Some of the pagans too. Is it right for us to listen to them, rabbi?'

Is it right? A boy he had taught since childhood waited for his answer. It was his duty to give it. But he stood silent.

'You must give the people a lead.' The merchant's voice echoed his own thoughts. 'Forgive me, rabbi, but you must. A rumour like this will spread like fire unless quenched at once. It will divide the people and they will not know which way to follow.'

He must speak. His voice came hesitantly. 'If I could find out by whose authority they spread this . . . this rumour. It may come from the temple.'

'But didn't he say that the rulers of the temple were the ones who had rejected the Messiah?' broke in the young man. The merchant winced at the word, but the boy didn't take any notice. 'It was the rulers in Jerusalem, wasn't it, who handed him over to be executed?'

'So you see,' said the merchant triumphantly, 'there is division already. Even in Jerusalem it seems. We mustn't let it happen here. Here where we are so few.' He drew even closer to the rabbi and took him by the arm. 'You must come down—forgive me if I appear to dictate to you, my rabbi—you must come down strongly on one side.'

But which side? It was as if the two voices were the voices of his conscience. He spoke his thought aloud. 'On one side or the other.'

The merchant uttered a horrified gasp, but the boy's voice rose in excitement.

'Then it may be true? It may be as the preacher said, that the time of deliverance has come.' He caught hold of his rabbi's hand and pleaded like a child. 'May I go, rabbi, may I go and hear what they have to tell us?'

'Rabbi!' It was a warning from the other side. The friendly hand on his arm became a steely grip. It was this that decided him. The trusting hand of the child seemed more important to him than the pressure of the man of influence. He turned towards the boy. 'Yes, you may go, my son.' He felt the grip on his arm relax and heard another horrified gasp. His voice regained its familiar authority as he spoke as a master to his pupil. 'But remember all you have been taught. Use your judgement and don't let yourself be carried away.' He watched the young man run out and heard him calling to his friends, 'The rabbi says yes... He says it may be true... There's no harm in listening, anyway.... Come on, which way did they go?' The voices died away. The rabbi made a decision. He moved towards the door. The merchant's voice snapped after him: 'Where are you going?'

'It is my duty to talk to these men.'

The hand was on his arm again. The voice in his ear. 'Speak to the people. You're the spiritual leader in this place. Assert yourself now, rabbi. Have these men run out of the town.'

In spite of his distress the rabbi's voice was firm. 'I shall take whatever action I consider necessary.' He pulled his arm away from the restraining grip and strode to the door, past a group of women who waited outside, and away up the now-deserted street. The merchant followed as far as the door, and stood with the women, looking after the retreating figure.

'Well, really!' complained a smartly dressed lady. 'I would have thought the rabbi would have something to say to us. I particularly wanted to speak to him.'

'He doesn't know what to make of it, that's the trouble,' said the merchant who was ruffled and not a little put out that the rabbi had not listened to his advice. 'He's got to assert his authority quickly, as I told him. But he's soft, you know. I mean no disrespect, but like a lot of these men of learning he can't make up his mind in an emergency.'

He found himself surrounded, the only male among these worried women.

'But what is one to think?'

'Why were these men allowed to come and speak such blasphemous nonsense?'

'In the synagogue of all places!'

'What did you make of it, sir?'

The last question came from a frail little woman at his elbow. He began to enjoy himself. 'Sheer nonsense, of course. And wicked nonsense, too. The rabbi should have stopped the speaker as soon as he started on this Messiah talk. Now all the young people are roused and excited, and if we're not very careful a new "cult" will be formed. Well, if it does it must be outside the synagogue. We must be sure of that.'

'I don't know what my husband will say,' said a rich Gentile proselyte. 'He was against my adopting the Jewish faith from the first. But if he hears of *this*. . .'

The rich merchant warmly agreed with this lady of influence.

'That's right,' he said. 'That's the way it will be. We who hold the true faith will be made to look ridiculous. We shall lose all those people we had won for the Lord God.'

'Well, the rabbi will certainly lose my support if he encourages this kind of thing,' said the lady firmly, feeling every bit as important and righteous as the merchant. 'What attracted me about your faith from the beginning was its solidity, its unchangingness. One God, one faith, one Law. But if we're going

to allow these strange ideas of men rising from the dead...
"Believe in this man and you will be saved" ... all that sort of
thing to creep in, well it will be no different from the pagans
who are for ever following strange gods as the fancy takes
them.'

The little woman who was a Jewess asked. 'You don't think
there could be any truth in it?'

The rich merchant, a man of her own race, looked down on
her condescendingly. 'My dear lady, I'm a business man and,
although I say it myself, I know how to do business. I know the
right time and the right way to go about things. Well, with all
due respect and meaning no irreverence, I would not expect
less of the Lord God than I would of myself.' He paused to let
the women take in this extraordinary and daring pronounce-
ment. They stared at him waiting for the next pearl of wisdom
to drop from his lips. He drew a deep breath and addressed
them all. 'Do you suppose that God, the all powerful and
almighty Lord, would choose such a way to send his chosen
people their Messiah? Unheard of except by his immediate
neighbours, arrested as an impostor by God's own priests in
Jerusalem, and executed as a criminal? What, with all due
reverence, would be the point of it?' There were respectful
murmurs of agreement, but the little woman persisted.

'But they say he rose from the dead.'

'They say, they say!' The rich man turned on her irritably.
'Can't you see that it's nothing but lies and rumours?' She did
not answer this rhetorical question, but continued to look at
him inquiringly. There was a note of exasperation in his voice
as he continued. 'Maybe these fanatics who followed him when
he was alive did really believe that he was the Messiah. Then he
was put to death. They couldn't bear to own that they had been
deceived, so they invented this story.'

'But why should they?' Her voice was timid and the look he
gave her should have forbidden further questions, but she had
had no satisfactory answer and her wondering made her bold.
'I mean, why should they come all this way to tell such an
extraordinary story unless it was ...'

She blushed and corrected herself '. . . unless they believed it to be true?'

The rich lady had had enough of this tiresome argument, and before the merchant could think of a sufficiently crushing reply she raised her voice. It was a piercing voice, one that demanded to be heard: 'Whether they believe it to be true or not is neither here nor there. The point is that such teaching has no place in the synagogue.' She included both the Jews in her withering look and the sweeping gesture of her hand. 'Unless I have entirely misunderstood all I have been taught.'

The business man who knew the right way to go about things knew also how to keep his customers. He turned to this one and his look of admiration was not wholly feigned. 'You're perfectly correct. Absolutely right. I often say that you newcomers to the faith grasp the truth of things better than some of us who have been brought up in it.' He glared at the little woman to let these words have their effect before he continued. 'Not that we don't believe that the Messiah will come—we look forward to that day no less eagerly than our ancestors did. I'd be the first to say so. But when he comes it will be with miracles and wonders. There will be no doubt in the mind of any true believer. He will come in glory and angels will herald him. He won't depend on a travel-stained tent-maker to tell the story at second-hand.' He was pleased with this speech. It seemed to put the whole matter neatly in a nutshell. He could scarcely believe his ears when the timid voice beside him persisted again.

'But there are different kinds of miracles and wonders. It's like he said, that bit of the scriptures he quoted at the end. . . "Such wonders I am doing in your days that if a man told you the story you would not believe him".'

She looked round the circle of faces. They were all glaring at her in silence as though she had said something indecent and, suddenly embarrassed by her own boldness, she blushed and hurried away. The merchant looked after her coldly then turned to his lady ally. 'You see how it takes them? The women, with all due respect to you, madam, the women and young people will be the worst. We'll have to take matters into our own hands. If the rabbi won't act we can call a meeting of the leading citizens. There's a lot of them, members of the synagogue, you know. We can put the whole thing on an official basis.' The business man was a loyal and public-spirited citizen. 'There's no room for trouble-makers in this town. I think I can make my colleagues join in drawing up a complaint. As long as we can keep them out of the synagogue there'll be no danger. They'll soon be laughed out of town by the Gentiles.'

So, in Iconium, as in other towns, the population was divided. Many listened to the teaching of the two apostles, but others, chiefly the leading citizens and influential Jews, accused them of blasphemy and sorcery and succeeded in having them driven from the town. Before they left Paul made one last public statement in the synagogue. 'We are brothers of the same race,' he said, 'and it was important that the word of God should be brought to you first. But since you reject it, we turn to the Gentiles.'

6
To the Gentiles

LYSTRA, although a Roman garrison town, was one of those cities that seemed to have been very little influenced by either Greek or Roman culture. The citizens were a sturdy, primitive, highland race, and only a very small minority of the population were Jews. Because they were so few, the Jews of Lystra clung to their faith and customs even more jealously than in the larger communities, but in spite of this there had been some intermarriage.

One such family was that of Eunice, a widow who lived with her mother, Lois, and her son Timothy. This young man had been brought up in the Jewish faith by his mother and grandmother, but because his father had been a Gentile he was watched with some suspicion by the neighbours in the little Jewish quarter in the town.

It was the day of the Feast of Jupiter and the streets and market-place were packed with holiday crowds. Among them, his eyes scanning the faces of the visitors from the surrounding villages, pushed Timothy. At last he came to the very edge of the town where the temple of Jupiter stood. He ran up the steps of the temple to get a better view.

'Peace be with you, Timothy. Come to see the crowds?' The speaker was a crippled beggar who lay at the temple gates. Timothy had known him all his life, and a warm friendship existed between the old man and the boy who seemed drawn together by a common sense of deprivation. Timothy greeted him eagerly:

'I'm looking for two strangers. Jews coming from Iconium.'

'The preachers?'

'Yes. Have you heard them?' There was eagerness in Timothy's voice.

'They've been speaking in the market-place. I couldn't get so far so I came here. I reckon they'll come this way to catch the crowds.'

He drew Timothy down beside him and his next words were a whisper:

'See those men?' Timothy followed his glance and saw a stranger standing with a Jewish baker, one of his neighbours. 'They're on the look-out for them too,' whispered the old man. 'Afraid they'll corrupt the Jews. You'd better take care, son.'

Timothy turned back to his friend and gripped his arm.

'But haven't you heard? Their message is for the Gentiles too.'

The excitement in his voice was not lost on the beggar for he knew how hard life had been for his young friend. To be born of mixed parentage made a man an outcast. He was better off himself, he sometimes thought, born without the use of his legs. He patted the boy's hand reassuringly.

'But how'll they make themselves understood, Timothy? There's not many in this town know Greek, and what a day to choose, the Feast of Jupiter!'

'Here they come.' It was the stranger who spoke. Timothy jumped to his feet and saw two men walking towards them followed by a small crowd. He ran down the steps to meet them.

'Peace be with you, sirs. . .'

Immediately his arm was seized by the baker:

'I warn you, Timothy, have nothing to do with these men.'

Timothy shook himself free; but the other man placed himself between him and the two preachers, and addressed them in a voice of assumed authority:

'On behalf of the Jewish community in Lystra I order both of you to leave this town immediately.'

Timothy was furious, but one of the preachers, the smaller of the two, replied quietly:

'We obey the order given us by the Lord.'

The baker raised his voice, 'We don't want any of your blasphemies here.'

'There is no blasphemy,' said Paul. 'You yourself have read in the scriptures, "I will make you a light to the nations—so that all the world may be saved".'

The two Jews were silent. Timothy asked, 'What does it mean, sir?'

Paul turned to him and read the eagerness in the boy's face.

'You know the promise that was made to our ancestors that he would send a Saviour?' he asked. Timothy nodded. 'The promise has come true. God has sent his own Son to be the light of the world, and those who follow him will no longer walk in the dark. They will "run and not get weary, they will walk and not grow weak, they will rise on wings like eagles".'

Timothy felt the restraining hand on his arm again and a voice in his ear, 'Timothy, I warn you,' but he took no notice. The words of the preacher had kindled a flame of hope that could not be quenched, and for this moment nobody existed for him but the man who had spoken them.

'All of us, sir?' he asked. 'Gentiles too?'

'All men, to the furthest parts of the earth.'

The flame became a blaze, a fire that seemed to consume him and the boy heard his own voice shouting: 'Tell them. Tell these Gentiles now.'

Paul felt a rush of love and gratitude towards the young man. All his weariness seemed to slip away as, followed by Barnabas, he ran up the steps of the temple and turned to face the pagan crowd. He stretched out his arms and called out to them:

'We bring a message . . .' The men nearest the steps drew

nearer and the beggar, delighted to be in the front row, gazed up at Paul with the same hope and excitement that Timothy had shown.

'We bring a message to you who were once far away. God has destroyed the barrier that once stood between us and kept us apart. . .'

Word travelled through the crowds that something interesting was happening, and more and more people drifted towards the temple steps. Paul raised his voice to include them.

'. . . God has sent life and light to you who lived in darkness. His kingdom is open to you and to all men, for it is within his love that we breathe and move and live.'

Quite a big crowd had now collected, a crowd, perhaps, not fully understanding the words that were spoken, but aware that something good was being offered to them. But there was one man besides Timothy who understood everything that Paul had said, and he called out in a loud voice, 'I believe you, sir.'

Paul turned and looked down at the frail, twisted body and the face which shone with faith.

'Stand up then and walk!'

Not for a moment did the look of wonder and joy leave the man's face. He grasped the hand that was stretched out to him and felt the power and the love that Paul had spoken of pouring into his body as, for the first time in his life, he stumbled to his feet.

Timothy ran to support him as Paul released his hand. But the beggar stood upright and steady.

'I can stand.' It was a shout of triumph.

A wave of excitement spread through the crowd, and those at the back pushed forward to see the marvel that had taken place outside the temple of Jupiter. They stood in breathless wonder as the man whose legs had been useless walked three steps towards the preacher and knelt at his feet.

Suddenly the awed silence was broken by a shout: 'The gods have come down to us in the form of men—Jupiter and Mercury are with us.' The cry was taken up and then as one man the mass of people fell on their knees in front of the temple, and two boys ran up the steps with garlands of flowers which they hung round the necks of Paul and Barnabas and then bowed to them.

For a moment they stood there decked with flowers before the kneeling crowd, then their bewilderment turned to horror as the procession of the priest of Jupiter made its way through the crowds towards them. Two boys led the procession swinging their censers of incense, and behind them came the pagan priest; by one hand he led a great white ox garlanded with flowers, and in the other he carried a huge knife. They guessed what was happening, but Timothy put their fears into words. 'They think you are Jupiter and Mercury. They're bringing the ox to sacrifice to you,' Paul tore the garland from his neck and stepped forward. Immediately a great cry went up: 'Mercury! Mercury!'

Paul held out his arms and his voice rang out above the cries.

'Men of Lystra, what are you doing? Stop, stop!' The procession came to a halt in some confusion as the crowd were on their feet now, and pressing forward to hear the voice of 'Mercury,' the messenger of the gods. Paul spoke slowly and deliberately.

'Listen to me. We are human men with the same nature as yourselves. It is the living God who has healed this man. The whole point of what we have been saying to you is that you must turn away from your false gods to the one living God who made the earth and the sky and everything in them.'

They were quiet now and listening intently.

'In days gone by he allowed all nations to go their own ways, but even then he did not leave you alone. It is he, the one true God, who gives you the sun and the rain to bring you food from the earth. It is he who gives you life and strength. He who fills your hearts with joy. . .'

'He speaks of Jupiter.' The shout came from the priest. 'Mercury the messenger speaks of Jupiter. See how the great god Jupiter stands silent.'

All eyes turned towards the tall figure of Barnabas and with cries of ecstasy the people of Lystra fell on their knees again.

'Stop!' Barnabas's usually quiet voice was a roar.

'Jupiter speaks!' cried the priest in an ecstasy of joy.

Barnabas stepped forward and looked down with compassion at the extraordinary scene that he and Paul had unwittingly provoked. With great deliberation he too tore the garland from his neck and addressed them.

'You fools. You ignorant men. Can't you understand? There is no Jupiter. No Mercury. No other god but the one living God whom no man has seen, but whose works are all round you. We are his witnesses. . .'

'False witnesses!' This time the interruption came from the merchant who had been awaiting his opportunity to work on the feelings of the highly emotional crowd and sway them to serve his purpose. He strode up the steps and turned to face them.

'Men of Lystra, these men whom you call "gods" are renegade *Jews* who have been driven from town to town because of their evil preaching. They are possessed by evil spirits, and by sorcery they have bewitched you. Look at them again. Do they look like gods?'

It was easier than he had hoped. A ripple of laughter was heard from the back, and some of the worshippers rose to their feet, looking now with hostility at the two shabby figures of the men they had taken for gods. Because they felt stupid they wanted revenge. The Jew was quick to sense the mood.

'These men are your enemies,' he proclaimed. 'Nothing but corruption can come to your people if you listen to these servants of the evil one. They come to destroy, to pervert, to practise magic and witchcraft among you. Save yourselves, men of Lystra, save yourselves before it is too late, and drive these men from your city.'

His words had just the effect he had anticipated, and with sickening anxiety Timothy heard the words that had terrified him since childhood, the slogan certain to fire men with anger: 'They are Jews.'

An ugly murmur ran through the crowd as they took up the cry, adding to it the other familiar accusation that gave their hatred the flavour of righteous indignation: 'They insult the gods!'

Timothy spoke urgently to Paul.

'You'd better come home with me, when these festival crowds are roused anything can happen.'

'I'll come with you that far,' said the beggar, very proud of his new strength. 'If they try to touch you they'll have to reckon with me.'

As the four of them descended the steps, the baker grabbed Timothy by the arm, and warned him. 'If you have anything to do with these men you will be ex-communicated. Your mother and grandmother too!'

Timothy pulled himself roughly from the man's grasp, striking him accidentally in the face as he did so. The baker staggered back.

'Come, sirs, quickly,' cried Timothy, and they pushed their way into the crowd, followed by the angry voice of the Jew, calling 'Stop them. They are dangerous. They are violent.'

His voice was lost in the confusion of sound, for now the priest and his procession were making their way towards the gates, and above the shouts of the crowd rose the voice of one of the retinue: 'Clear the way for the priest of Jupiter.' Two men armed with cudgels pushed their way into the mob and began to hit out at those who impeded the progress of the procession.

With raised cudgel one of the men turned on Paul, but a push from the beggar turned the blow aside. The other man rushed at Paul and struck him on the head. He was tackled at once by Barnabas, and while Paul lay motionless on the ground his three friends were caught up in a fierce struggle, with the crowd yelling around them. A real fight had begun and Barnabas, Timothy and the beggar were carried far from Paul by the angry, jostling crowd.

Stunned by the blow from the cudgel, Paul was only dimly aware of the priest's procession which passed close to him and when at last he raised his head a drunken man picked up a stone, and threw it a him. Paul lay still, face downwards.

The procession moved on, and with it the crowd, their feet stirring the dust into a cloud behind them. The street was empty, except for the still figure of Paul. But not for long. The two Jews, who had retreated up the steps out of the way of the mob, walked slowly towards him. With his foot the merchant turned Paul over on his back. He lay stiff and motionless, his head bloody, his face bruised and streaked with dust.

The two men looked at each other—a look of satisfaction. Then they walked down the silent street.

Suddenly across the empty square came the sound of running. Panting and dishevelled, Barnabas, Timothy and the beggar rushed to the still form of Paul. They knelt round his body, and Barnabas, his face bleeding from the fight, put his hand on Paul's heart.

'Is he dead?' asked Timothy; Barnabas didn't answer but called his friend's name—'Paul, Paul.'

Paul's eyelids flickered, and at last he opened his eyes and looked up at Barnabas.

His voice came in a whisper. 'What was it Stephen said? "Lord, do not hold this sin against them".'

As they approached Timothy's home, his mother was horrified at first when she saw her son in such company, for all of them were torn and dirty. But she put a mattress on the floor for Paul, and when he had been lifted on to it, fetched water so that Barnabas could wash his wounds.

Later that day, when darkness had fallen and Barnabas had gone out, Timothy's old grandmother, Lois, asked querulously how long these strangers were to stay.

'Ssh, mother,' said Eunice, looking towards the corner where Timothy knelt beside Paul. 'Only till tomorrow they say, though that one doesn't seem fit enough to travel thirty miles to Derbe.'

Lois protested that her daughter was putting them all in danger by having them in the house. 'It's not only the Jews, but the whole town's against them.'

'That's nothing to the joy there is in having them here,' said Eunice softly.

'Joy?' the old woman snapped. 'A lot of extra trouble I'd say.'

'Ssh,' said Eunice again. 'Timothy's the one I'm thinking of. He's a different boy even after one day with Paul. It's like having a father again.' And, seeing that Paul was stirring, she rose to prepare a meal for him.

Under her care, and Timothy's, Paul was indeed well enough to leave next day. Timothy was sad to part from him.

'Timothy, my son,' said Paul, 'think about the things we have talked over; run your best in the race of faith, and keep your faith with a clear conscience. Pray at all times that everyone may be saved and come to know the truth.'

'But you'll come back to us, won't you?' asked Timothy, and on being reassured went on, 'I wish I could go with you. Do you think the brotherhood would accept me even though I'm half-Greek and uncircumcised?'

'My son,' said Paul, "the message of Christ is for everyone who believes.'

Not long afterwards, in the upstairs room in Jerusalem, a formal council was gathered. Peter and John were there, and so was James the Just who, with some heat, was addressing them.

'Unless a man follows the whole law of Moses,' he insisted, 'he cannot be saved. If a Gentile is converted to believe in Jesus the Messiah, then he must be circumcised, as a Jew is. We cannot have division in the brotherhood—circumcised and uncircumcised—those who know the Law and those who are ignorant of it.'

Encouraged by the murmur of agreement which greeted his words, he said that in Antioch, where the brotherhood called themselves Christians, they learnt that there were more Gentiles than Jews.

'They accept Jesus as the Christ, but they know nothing about our Law,' he went on indignantly. 'They eat and drink as pagans still. And even worse, the Jewish Christians there are becoming lax, eating and drinking with the Gentile brethren—forgetting the laws of our ancestors.'

At once John was on his feet.

'Brothers,' he said, 'remember our Lord's words when he prayed for us, "I pray not only for them, but also for those who believe in me because of their message. I pray that they may all be one. Father! May they be in us, just as you are in me and I am in you".'

James struck the table with his hand as he protested, 'But one—within the Law. . .'

John sat down; and immediately Peter stood up and asked if they were not forgetting that already they had broken away from the Law and accepted Gentiles, and that indeed the church in Antioch was not the first to do so.

'Remember the Ethiopian that Philip baptized,' he said, 'and the Centurion Cornelius. God has plainly shown that the Gentiles should hear the word and should believe it. It is because of their *faith* that God has given them the Holy Spirit, just as he gave it to us. Therefore, why should we put the extra burden of the Law on them? It is not the Law but faith in the Lord that has saved us—Jew and Gentile alike.'

There was dead silence as he sat down. And then realizing that Paul and Barnabas were present, James rose to suggest that they should tell them of their experiences in the pagan cities.

Barnabas spoke first. 'Brothers,' he said, 'wherever we went we preached first to the Jews, but in town after town they turned us from their synagogues, while the pagans begged us to tell them the news we had brought. Who were we to turn our backs on men who were searching for God?'

'And what did you preach to these pagans?' asked James.

Paul rose to answer him. 'The gospel that we preached,' he explained, 'was faith in Christ Jesus. For, as Peter has said, it was not by keeping the Law that we Jews received the Holy Spirit. It was by faith in the living Christ. Before his coming we were all imprisoned under the power of the Law, and none more than I. But now I am dead to the Law and live for God, who is the God of both Jews and Gentiles. I preached that all who have faith in Christ are the sons of God. There is no distinction between Jew and Greek, slave and free man, male and female. All are one in Christ.'

James was impressed by Paul's words, but still troubled. He asked if Paul meant that the law of Moses should count for nothing so long as men had faith.

'No,' Paul replied, 'but faith comes first. We do not undermine the Law. We put it in its proper place.'

As he sat down, James, his mind made up, rose to address the gathering again.

'Brothers,' he said, 'I can see that we must compromise. From what Peter, Paul, and Barnabas have said, it seems clear that we should not put any fresh difficulties in the way of these Gentiles who are turning to God. We must rather strengthen and encourage them. But I think we should send letters to Antioch and the other churches where there are Gentiles, reminding them of the main points of the Law which must be observed, but telling them that we, in Jerusalem, do not insist that Gentiles must be circumcised.'

They all agreed, and at once began to prepare a carefully worded letter which Paul and Barnabas took with them to Antioch. There they handed it to Silas, who read it aloud to the Gentile Christians.

Silas read:

From the apostles and brotherhood in Jerusalem to the brothers who are Gentiles in Antioch of Syria—GREETINGS

Our dear brothers Paul and Barnabas, who have risked their lives for the sake of our Lord Jesus Christ, return to you with this message.

It has been decided to place no further burden on you except what is absolutely necessary within the Law: avoid food that has been offered to idols and the flesh of animals that have been strangled, and do not become involved with anything immoral.

Do this and you will prosper.   *FAREWELL*

Paul watched as the Gentiles crowded round Silas, exclaiming with joy and relief at this decision which allowed men to become Christians without first becoming Jews. Then he turned to Barnabas and said that they must carry this news to the churches in Asia they had visited.

Barnabas's eyes were on Mark, who stood near them.

'I'd like to take him with me,' he said quietly; but Paul said, 'No'. Mark had deserted them once, and there was no room for anyone so faint-hearted in missionary work. 'In Lystra,' he pointed out, 'the lad Timothy wants to join us. He would be a better assistant.'

'But Mark has changed,' urged Barnabas, and he called his nephew to join them. 'Now that the brotherhood in Jerusalem have given this decision about the Gentiles, Mark is eager to work for us. Isn't that so, Mark?'

'Yes, let me come with you, Paul,' begged Mark. 'I'm ready now. I understand now.'

But Paul was firm. He said he was sorry, but it would not do. He must have men he could trust.

'Then,' said Barnabas, 'we must go different ways.' He was determined that he and Mark should stay together. And so, after their long friendship, Paul and Barnabas parted, and Paul set out on his next journey with Silas of Antioch as his companion.

They travelled across the sea and over the mountains back to Lystra, where they were welcomed by Timothy and his mother. Even when Eunice learnt that Paul wanted Timothy to join him in his work, she consented willingly. She went with them to the gates of the town, and there she embraced her son and said farewell.

Paul, Silas and Timothy travelled many miles together, carrying the letters to Gentile Christians, until at last they came to the port of Troas on the western shores of Asia. And there Paul fell ill with malaria. Timothy cared for him devotedly, and when Paul became despondent, wondering if he had been foolish to come to Troas, instead of following his own in-clinations and going to Ephesus, it was Timothy who reminded him that it was the Spirit of Jesus which had led them to this place on the coast.

But Timothy was worried by Paul's doubts and misgivings,

thinking they were due to his fever. He decided to consult Silas, and went out to look for him. In the courtyard of the inn where they had their lodgings the innkeeper, Carpus, was busy sweeping; and sitting in the shadow was a stranger, dressed in the Greek style, his cape and a large brimmed hat beside him. He was engrossed in what he was doing—writing on a scroll. In his anxiety Timothy scarcely noticed him. The innkeeper told him that Silas had gone out early, and asked how Paul was.

'He's ill,' said Timothy, glad to share his troubles with someone. 'Very ill, I think. He seems to be delirious.'

Carpus pointed to the Greek stranger. 'Well, there's a man who might help you. He's a doctor from Macedonia, often stays here.'

Timothy went over to him. The doctor looked up from his work.

'Peace be with you,' said Timothy hastily, and then poured out his tale: his friend was ill. Would the doctor come in and see him?

The Greek rose to his feet at once.

'Take me to him,' he said.

Paul lay tossing on his bed, muttering.

As Timothy and the doctor entered, they caught the words: 'Where? . . . Where should I go, Lord? Show me the way . . . Don't let me fail you, Lord. . .'

The doctor signalled to Timothy to leave him alone with Paul, and then he sat beside him and squeezed some herbs into a cup of water.

Paul opened his eyes and stared at him: 'Who are you?'

'My name is Luke, I am a doctor.'

Luke made Paul drink the liquid from the herbs, then examined him and bathed his chest. He assured Paul that he was not as ill as Timothy had suggested—it was no more than a slight fever.

'You've travelled far?' he asked.

'From Antioch in Syria, through Cilicia and across Asia,' replied Paul.

'You are Jewish preachers, aren't you? I heard something of

your work when I was in Antioch. Christians, I believe they call
you?'

When Paul told him this was so, he asked how it was that he
had come to Troas where there were even fewer of his race than
in Antioch.

This was the very thought which had been troubling Paul,
but he would not voice it to a stranger. Instead he said briefly,
'The message we carry is for everyone.'

'What is the message?' asked Luke.

Paul looked directly at him. 'For the Gentiles, that they
should turn from their false gods to the one true God who is
the maker of everything.'

'The Hebrew religion, in fact. All of us have heard of your
one all-powerful and invisible God. And of your Law. Did you
find many who would turn from the gods they know to one so
remote and so exacting?'

'He is not remote,' Paul assured him. 'He is within the reach
of everyone.'

'And what of this other one,' asked Luke earnestly. 'The one
they call the Christ?'

'He is the visible expression of the one invisible God,' said
Paul.

'You believe that he will come soon and change the world?'
Luke asked. 'Is that what you preach?'

'He has come, and he is changing the world.'

'Where is he?'

'Everywhere.'

Luke wondered whether Paul was indeed delirious, and he
put his hand on his brow. Paul seized it, and began to talk with
some of his old assurance and strength.

'Listen, Luke,' he said eagerly. 'He came as a man to the people of Galilee and Judea. He lived among them and taught that
men should love each other, should feed the hungry, heal the
sick, and worship God wholeheartedly; and he promised that
God would send his Spirit to the human race and that this
Spirit would never leave them . . . It is this Spirit that is alive in
us today—this Spirit that is turning the pagans from their false

gods. Don't you see, it is no longer a question of Jews telling Gentiles that theirs is the true God, but the living Spirit of Christ being poured out on everyone who believes in him.'

Luke was impressed by the sincerity and the eagerness of Paul's tone.

'A universal God,' he said wonderingly. 'A universal Spirit. Yes, I could believe that,' he went on, excitement growing in his voice. 'A God of love who cared for the hungry and the sick, the slaves, the people who live in fear. In my country they are like sheep without a shepherd, so many gods to serve. Even the emperor has made himself into a god and demands worship and sacrifice.'

Suddenly he turned to Paul and spoke with urgency. 'Paul, cross over to Macedonia and help us.'

But Paul, appeared to have fallen asleep. Luke felt his brow, covered him up and went out, leaving Paul to his dreams. Paul had heard all that Luke had said. And in his feverish half-sleep he saw in his mind's eye the Greek gods: Zeus, Hermes and Apollo; and the Roman gods: Liber and Sylvanus. He saw too the Emperor Augustus, in all his pomp and power. Then he saw the sea, and beyond it on the shore Luke beckoning to him, and calling, 'Cross over to Macedonia and help us.' With Luke's voice in his ears he drifted into sound sleep.

When he woke next day he was his old eager and energetic self again. He got up and, having dressed, went into the court-yard to find Timothy, who was watching Luke writing. He was writing, he said, the things Paul had told him the previous night about the Christ.

'Timothy, my son,' said Paul, 'go down to the harbour and find out how soon there is a ship sailing for Macedonia.'

'Are you better, master?' asked Timothy.

'Quite better,' replied Paul. 'Now I know where we are going.'

As Timothy ran off to the harbour, Paul turned to Luke and took hold of him.

'Luke,' he said, 'I am going to Macedonia to help your people.'

7
Greece

PAUL, Timothy and Silas, with their new friend Luke, sailed from Troas to Macedonia in northern Greece.

Luke was on familiar ground and led the way through the flat countryside, pointing out landmarks to them, finding the best places for them to rest when they were weary, until at last they reached the outskirts of Philippi, the chief city in this part of Macedonia. It was an impressive place with its Roman forum, Greek temples, statues of Roman gods and its colonnaded streets.

Timothy could have explored all day, but they had work to do and lodgings to find. Paul was anxious to give his message to the people, and on the sabbath they went to the banks of the River Gangites, where they had heard there was a place of prayer. Most of his listeners were women, and among them was Lydia, a trader in dyed cloth. With all her household she was baptized. Afterwards she insisted that all four of them should stay in her house in Philippi.

Its biggest room was both shop and workroom, stacked high with bales of coloured cloth. More coloured cloth hung outside, where a sign over the door also indicated her profession.

Timothy soon tried his hand at the dye bath, stirring the steaming liquid with a stick and every now and then raising a piece of cloth to see how the colour was taking. Lydia smiled at his enjoyment, then went over to speak to Luke who was writing on a tablet.

'What are you writing?' she asked.

'About you,' said Luke, with a smile, and he showed her what he had written. It seemed to be a diary and he had put down all about the meeting on the banks of the River Gangites, and how she had been baptized, and had brought them all back to stay in her home. She blushed with pleasure to see herself mentioned, and asked Luke if he wrote everything down.

'Yes,' Luke assured her. 'I'm going to put the whole journey on record: everything that happens to us. And the things that happened when Jesus was in Galilee—I mean to find out about that too.'

'You're giving yourself a lot of work,' said Lydia with a laugh, then she turned back to her work.

'Where are Paul and Silas?' asked Luke.

'They went with Timothy and me to the market-place to buy a bale of cloth, but we left them there. There's a young fortune-telling girl who keeps bothering them—calling out after them, you know. I advised them to avoid her, but Paul thinks she is possessed by a devil. He seems to think he can help her.'

'Possessed by a devil, or sick in mind—it is the same thing. Maybe I could help,' said Luke, and putting away his writing he went out to find his friends.

When he found them, Paul and Silas were standing watching the antics of a slave girl who was dancing, surrounded by a small crowd. She was about twelve years old—a thin, pale child with staring eyes. Her master, a prosperous-looking man, stood near her, a whip in his hand. The girl writhed about with strange snake-like movements, but at the end of her dance she collapsed on the ground and lay still. A man pushed to the front of the crowd and threw down some coins.

'Prophesy, prophesy,' he said.

The girl rose on to her knees, her eyes wide open. She

stretched out her thin little arms and began to speak in a strange unnatural voice.

'The servant of the great god Apollo speaks . . .' she intoned. 'You will have a good health and a long life.'

A second man gave some money to the girl's master and called out to her, 'What does the great Apollo say to me?'

Her master flicked the girl's shoulders with the whip and repeated the question. The girl rose, ran over to the man and clutched his arm.

'Those you love will prosper, those you hate will die,' she said; and of her own accord she ran up to a third man and called out to him in her strange harsh voice, 'This man the great Apollo calls to be his servant. He will have the power to heal or the power to strike dead.'

Some of the crowd cheered and congratulated the man, who threw a handful of silver to the master; but Paul and Silas were appalled by what they had seen.

'Who is she? Did Lydia tell you?' asked Silas, and Paul told him that she was the orphan child of Jewish parents, sold into slavery when they died. Her master made a good living from her tricks.

At that moment the girl's master saw them, and thinking that they were potential customers, called out, 'Money, good strangers, money for the prophecies of Apollo!'

Paul showed no sign of having heard the man, who continued to cajole.

'She'll tell the future for you, sirs,' he said. 'The servant of Apollo, possessed with divine powers.'

Suddenly the girl ran over and clung to Paul, crying out in a loud voice, 'These men are servants of the Highest God. They can tell us a way of salvation.'

Gently Paul removed her hands, but she threw herself on the ground in front of him, still crying out that they were servants of the Highest God. Then she began to beat hysterically on the ground with her fists, crying and screaming, 'Tell us the way of salvation. Tell us the way of salvation . . .'

Paul looked down at her with compassion, then spoke

quietly and with great authority.

'Evil spirit, in the name of Jesus Christ, I command you to come out of her.'

The girl gave a little whimpering sob and then lay quiet. After a second she raised her head and looked round, not knowing where she was. Her master pushed forward angrily. He raised his whip, and shouted at her, 'Prophesy, prophesy in the name of Apollo.'

She looked at him in terror and bewilderment, then cowered away from him, hiding her face. He turned angrily to Paul. 'What Jewish trick is this?' he demanded.

'He used the name of a new god ... Jesus Christ,' said someone in the crowd.

'Men of Philippi,' said Paul earnestly, 'listen to me. There is only one God, maker of everything and there is only one Saviour, Jesus Christ, in whose name I cast the devil out of this child.'

'Devil?' shouted the girl's master in fury. 'Devil? She was appointed by Apollo to be his servant.'

Luke made his way purposefully through the crowd.
'You mean,' he said, 'you used her suffering to spread your lies and make money for yourself.'

He bent over the little girl, taking her hand and speaking to her quietly. There were indignant shouts from the master and some of the crowd.

Luke picked the child up in his arms, murmuring to her that it was all right and that no one was going to hurt her.

'Put her down!' roared her master. 'I'll beat some sense into her.'

'She's coming home with me,' said Luke firmly.

'What?' protested the man. 'You can't do that. I'll have the law on you. The girl belongs to me. I paid good money for her.'

'She's made more money for you than you ever gave for her,' said Luke, to which the man retorted that it was none of Luke's business.

'It is my business,' said Luke firmly. 'I am a doctor and this child is ill.'

The man turned to the crowd for support. 'If she's ill,' he said, 'it's because this man here has cast a spell on her. Witchcraft, that's what it is. I'll have the law on him. You see if I don't. We're very strict in this town about things like that.'

Silas told him bluntly that he had better be careful of the law himself. The man was less sure of his ground now, and looked agitated. He knew his living was gone, but he knew too that it was an illegal living, since no witchcraft or sorcery was allowed in the streets. But now as he watched Luke push his way through the crowd with the girl in his arms, to take her home with him to Lydia, he turned blusteringly to the crowd again.

'Gentlemen,' he said, 'you'll be my witnesses. You all saw what happened. The girl was fit and strong before these two Jews came on the scene and cast a spell on her. We've had trouble before with Jews in this city, taking our living away, insulting our gods and our emperor. Are we going to allow it to happen again?'

There was an indignant growl from the men standing round, and they began to move threateningly towards Paul and Silas. But Paul spoke calmly.

'We do not insult your emperor. He, too, is a servant of the living God.'

The girl's master saw his chance. 'The emperor a *servant*,' he echoed. 'He's condemned himself by his own words,'

Paul stood his ground, maintaining that the man was in danger of the law for employing the child as a soothsayer. But the listeners were easily influenced by the furious and frightened man, and shouting that Paul and Silas should be taken to court, they seized them and dragged them off down the street.

That night while the slave girl lay on a made-up bed, watching Lydia light the lamps, Timothy, who had been to the court, told Luke the bitter tale. There had been no proper trial, no chance to defend themselves. The magistrates had taken the word of the girl's employer that Paul and Silas had been practising witchcraft, had insulted the emperor and tried to persuade the people to pay tribute to a 'foreign god'.

'I should have warned them,' said Lydia, reproaching herself in her distress. 'It's not safe for a Jew to make himself conspicuous in this town. They'll seize on any excuse to stamp them out. If only they'd come home with me.'

'I couldn't get near them when the lictors dragged them out of the court,' said Timothy. 'A huge crowd had collected. It was horrible. They were more like beasts than men.' He shuddered violently at the memory, and Luke stopped his pacing and sat beside him.

'How did they take it?' he asked. 'Did you see them when . . .?'

'Yes, I saw them,' said Timothy. 'They were tied to a pillar . . . and stripped to the waist. Then the lictors—there were four of them—flogged them. I thought it would go on forever . . . and at every stroke the crowd let out a roar of delight—as though they were watching some kind of entertainment.'

He was trembling with grief and rage. Luke laid his hand on his arm, and asked how Paul and Silas bore it.

'They never made a sound,' said Timothy. 'Though their backs were torn and bleeding—they were raw, Luke, quite raw—I didn't hear a single cry. I saw them again as they were being taken to the jail.'

'They were able to walk?' Luke asked, and when Timothy said they had had to, they were driven like cattle, he said how much he wished he could go to them. 'I'm a doctor,' he added. 'Maybe they'd let me in to dress the wounds.'

Timothy shook his head. 'No,' he said. 'I tried. The prison governor himself has been put in charge of them. Nobody's to be allowed near them tonight.'

There was silence for a while, then Lydia went to a window and threw it open.

'How hot it is,' she said. 'Hot and still. Feels like a storm.'

For the first time the girl on the bed spoke, and now it was a normal child's voice, not the hoarse cry of the market-place.

'It feels like it did before the earthquake,' she said.

'Earthquake?' asked Lydia, surprised.

'My mother and father were killed in an earthquake, you know,' said the girl. 'I was very small, but I remember it felt like this before . . .'

Meanwhile in the town jail Paul and Silas were closely guarded. The two guards on duty in the courtyard outside their cells grumbled to each other about the heat and the airlessness of the night, then sprang to attention and saluted as the governor came from his house nearby. He was a Roman officer, a centurion. Having made sure that all was in order, he took off his helmet and mopped his brow. And at that moment he heard the sound of singing. Astonished, he crossed to the cells and peered through the grille. Through it came the words of the psalm that Paul and Silas sang:

> Give thanks to the Lord, because he is good,
>   and his love is eternal.
> The stone which the builders rejected as worthless
>   turned out to be the most important of all.
> This was done by the Lord;
>   what a wonderful sight it is!
> May God bless the one who comes
>   in the name of the Lord!
> Give thanks to the Lord, because he is good,
>   and his love is eternal.

The governor stepped back from the grille, and looked questioningly at the guards, but they only shrugged their shoulders and grinned. For a moment the governor hesitated, and it looked as if he was going to open the cell and go in, but he turned instead and went to his house.

That night when he went to bed the governor could not get the two Jewish prisoners out of his mind. As he unbuckled his breast-plate he told his wife about them, and that he had heard them singing. One line stayed in his mind: 'May God bless the one who comes in the name of the Lord'. He leaned out of the window, and listened intently, but everywhere was silent now.

In the small, crowded cell nearby Paul and Silas, their feet in stocks, endured the suffocating heat. The livid weals on their backs reminded them of the flogging they had suffered, and made it painful for them to lean back on the wall behind them. They looked with pity at their fellow prisoners, some of whom sat with their heads between their knees trying to sleep. One man with a scarred and brutish face who lay with his head on the stocks asked for another song. 'It passes the time,' he said.

Though he was exhausted by his ordeal, Silas began to sing, and Paul joined in, while one after another the prisoners raised their heads to listen.

> *God is our shelter and strength,*
> > *always ready to help in times of trouble.*
> *So we will not be afraid, even if the*
> > *earth is shaken*
> *and mountains fall into the ocean depths;*
> > *even if the seas roar and rage,*
> > *and the hills are shaken by the violence.*

The sound of their voices woke the governor as he lay beside his sleeping wife; and now in the silence of night he could hear the comforting words:

> *'Stop fighting,' he says, 'and know that I am God,*
> *supreme among the nations,*
> *supreme over the world.'*
> *The Lord Almighty is with us;*
> *the God of Jacob is our refuge.*

There was silence for a moment, and then, a distant ominous rumble, followed by the roar of falling masonry. The house shook, some jars fell off a shelf, and the window shutter which had been wide open to let in the air crashed shut, leaving the room in darkness. The governor leapt out of bed, and his wife woke and screamed in terror.

'Lights, bring lights!' the governor called, groping his way towards the door. The rumbling noise continued like thunder, and there was confused shouting from the guards and the prisoners.

A moment later a guard stumbled into the room, the flickering light of his torch lighting up his panic-stricken face.

'Are you all right, sir?' he managed to ask.

The governor seized his sword, and then snatched the torch from the guard, with a stern order to him to get back on duty. In the deathly silence which had suddenly followed the roar of the earthquake, the governor and the guard dashed from the house to the prisoners' cell. The door stood wide open. Inside was pitch dark. There was no sound.

'Who opened the door?' asked the governor.

'It was the shock of the earthquake, sir,' said the guard.

The governor was appalled. He knew that to lose his prisoners meant disgrace, and that it would be better to die by his own hand. He raised his sword, the point towards his heart. 'No, no!' His wife rushed from the house and threw herself at his feet, clinging to him and holding the arm that held the sword.

'Hush, my love,' said the governor gently. 'You know the law. Better to die by my own hand than be stripped of honour.'

His wife sank down weeping, as he raised the sword again, but from the darkness of the cell came a shout.

'Don't hurt yourself. We are all here.' It was the voice of Paul.

'Bring a light,' cried the governor, and when it was brought he could see by its wavering light Paul and Silas standing there in the cell, the chains fallen from them. Behind them the other prisoners stood in a group, dumb with terror.

The guard, his courage rapidly returning, counted them briskly.

'That's right, sir—none missing,' he said.

The governor swayed on his feet, and leaned against the wall for support, as he ordered the guard to bring the two Jews out into the courtyard. He did so, then closed the cell door as well as he could, for the earthquake had wrenched it from its frame. What was happening in the courtyard amazed him, for he saw the governor, a Roman centurion, fall trembling on his knees in front of Paul and Silas.

'Stand up,' said Paul. 'There's nothing to be afraid of.'

'Sirs,' asked the governor, 'is it true, what they say, that you are the servants of the Most High God?'

'Yes,' said Paul.

'What must I do to be . . . saved?' asked the governor.

His wife who had helped him to his feet and now stood beside him tried to comfort him. 'But you are saved,' she said. 'Saved from death.' But the governor still trembled and shook his head.

Paul looked directly at him, understanding his need.

'Believe in the Lord Jesus,' he said, 'and you and your family will be saved.'

'What does he mean?' asked the wife in a puzzled whisper.

Her husband told her to go indoors and prepare food and clothing for their guests, and water to wash their wounds; and still puzzled she obeyed and went into the house.

The governor turned to Paul and Silas, and warmly welcomed them to his home, begging them to tell him about their Lord.

In the bright sunshine of the next morning the townspeople were out looking at the havoc caused by the earthquake. Lydia's house had suffered little damage, though the sign outside her door had fallen to the ground, where it still lay among tiles from the roof. The little girl was busy sweeping dust and stones from the big workroom out into the street, while indoors Lydia and Timothy picked up an overturned work bench, and mopped up a pool of dye. From the yard a cock crowed, and the little girl, stopping her sweeping to admire him, suddenly saw a familiar figure in the street.

'Here he comes,' she called excitedly. 'Here comes the doctor.'

Lydia and Timothy stopped their work and hurried to the door to greet Luke, who could hardly wait to tell his news.

'Well, how were they? Did you manage to get in?' They flung

the questions at him.

'I got in,' he said, 'and spoke to the guard; he was quite friendly. The most amazing thing has happened.'

'What?' asked Timothy.

Lydia demanded to know if they were free.

'Free to go whenever they like.'

Timothy stared at him in astonishment. 'Well, why aren't they with you?'

'Wait while I tell you,' said Luke with a smile. 'In the first place, the prison governor, his family and whole household have been baptized.'

'*What?*' Timothy was incredulous, while Lydia murmured, 'God be praised.'

Luke explained that Paul and Silas were with the governor and his family in their home. They had been given food and fresh clothes, and it seemed that while they were at breakfast lictors had come from the magistrates with orders to the governor to release them.

'But why?' asked Timothy.

'The guard thinks the magistrates were scared by the earthquake coming so soon after their arrest. Thought there was a supernatural power at work. Anyway, they are anxious to get them out of the city.'

'But where are they now?' demanded Timothy.

'They refused to leave until the magistrates themselves came and made a formal apology. The guard said it was as good as a play to see Paul and Silas standing there beside the prison governor, dressed in Roman togas and declaring that as Roman citizens they had been shamefully and unlawfully treated. The lictors were really scared, it seems, and hurried off to report to the magistrates.'

'Will the magistrates go, do you think?' asked Timothy.

'I think it's possible,' said Luke. 'It's illegal for citizens to be flogged or to be imprisoned without trial. We must wait and see.'

And while in Lydia's house they finished clearing up the havoc of the earthquake, and then busied themselves with preparations for welcoming Paul and Silas, an extraordinary scene was taking place in the courtyard of the jail.

At the top of the steps leading down from the governor's house stood Paul and Silas, looking very different from the two prisoners in chains they had been the night before. They were dressed in togas belonging to the governor. Their lacerated backs had been skilfully tended. They had washed away the grime of prison, and had been well fed. They stood with dignity beside the governor and his wife, and the two guards in attendance. At the foot of the stairs, cringing and apologetic, were two magistrates.

'We are Roman citizens, yet you flogged us publicly,' said Paul sternly.

'Sirs, we did not know,' said one of the magistrates. 'We most humbly apologize.'

Paul declared that he and Silas had been imprisoned without any kind of trial, and that they had been given no chance to speak in their own defence.

'Sir, everything you say is true', said the other magistrate. 'We admit that as good men and citizens of Rome you have indeed been subjected to a great injustice. We most humbly apologize and beg your forgiveness.'

With great dignity Paul accepted their apology, and with relief the magistrates waited while Paul turned to the governor and shook him warmly by the hand. Then he and Silas took leave of the governor's wife, and of the two guards. As they came down the steps one of the magistrates stepped forward and asked politely where they were going.

'To our friends,' said Paul.

'For your own safety,' said the magistrate, 'I would advise you to leave the city at once. The law will do all in its power to protect you, but there are subversive elements, you understand, and it would be wise not to underestimate them.'

Paul made no comment. The magistrates bowed as they passed them, then scowled to see the governor and his wife and the two guards smiling and waving to Paul and Silas, who turned back to wave farewell at the prison gates.

There was great rejoicing at Lydia's house when they returned to it, but Paul and Silas agreed with Luke that it would be wise for them to leave almost at once. They took Timothy with them; but Luke stayed on in Lydia's house which became the meeting-place of the Christian brethren in Philippi. It was strange that the name Christian invented by unbelievers in Antioch, should have become the name by which they were best known—and there were now quite a large number of them.

For two months they heard nothing of Paul, and then one day Lydia hurried in in great excitement.

'A letter. . . A letter at last,' she called out, waving a scroll.

'From them?' asked Luke, and Lydia assured him it must be. Merchants from Berœa had brought it, and said it was given them by 'the son of a tent-maker' by the name of Timothy.

'From Berœa?' repeated Luke, as he took the scroll and un-rolled it. 'They've moved on.'

The girl, who was now healthy and happy in Lydia's care, ran up to listen as he began to read.

Paul, Silas and Timothy, servants of Christ Jesus to our sister Lydia, our dear doctor Luke and to Christ's family in Philippi,

GREETINGS

This letter comes to you from Berœa where we arrived from Thessalonica last week. Our stay there ended abruptly and it was with great reluctance that we left, but it was necessary to do so in order to protect the lives of our fellow Christians. As has so often happened in the past, Jews stirred up trouble against us and reported to the civic authorities, using the same charge that was made against our Lord himself. I quote the actual words: 'These men have turned the world upside down. They are traitors to Cæsar saying that there is another king called Jesus . . .' Enemies have followed us here to Berœa and after a night of prayer we have come to the parting of the ways of us three, for a time at least; since it is Paul whom the Jews are most determined to destroy, he is to leave the city today. Silas and I,

Timothy, are to remain here to guide the young church, and Paul is to travel south . . . to Athens.

Pray for us, brothers and sisters, and especially for our beloved Paul, who has been at all times like a father to us and now goes so far without his sons. He sent you this message: 'Remember how much I love you. The grace of our Lord Jesus Christ be with you.'

So Paul left the friends who had become so close to him, and took a ship sailing to Athens. He was alone now, with a mission to accomplish by himself.

Once in Athens he spent some time walking round the town taking in all he saw—the statues, temples and beautiful Acropolis among the olive and cypress trees, trying to adjust himself to these new surroundings, and to a new type of audience. He knew that he was in the cultural centre of the world, the artistic and intellectual capital, the stronghold of Greek mythology, the home of the greatest artists, poets, writers and orators the world had known. He realized the challenge of this city. How was he to speak of the kingdom of heaven to these Athenians who had made their own heaven on earth? How could he preach of a scourged and crucified God in a place where the greatest philosophers had taught that one should adore any man who possessed the beauty that was reflected in Phidias's statues?

As he looked at one after another of the beautiful statues of the pagan gods he realized again that he must be 'all things to all men'. Deep in thought, his attention was caught by a perfectly plain stone monument, and on it the inscription: 'To the Unknown God'. He repeated the words softly to himself. He had found his line of approach.

He quickened his step and found himself in the Agora, the colonnaded market-place in the centre of Athens. Here were stalls heaped with brightly coloured flowers, others displaying books or perfumes. The shouts of the slave traders proclaiming their human wares vied with those of the vendors selling figs from Caria, oysters from Chios, honey from Mount Hymettus. Against this babble of voices, there in the market-place, poets recited their doctrines, the followers of Plato expounded their theories about the transmigration of souls, and Stoics their noble philosophy of the quest for virtue. Here, too, were the Epicureans teaching boldly that the world was made by chance.

Paul mingled with the crowds, watching and listening, biding his time. He joined the throng round an Epicurean philosopher who was talking earnestly: 'Men of Athens, why are you forever trying to placate the gods, living in fear of them, hoping for their favours? Can you not understand that the gods whose statues adorn our city are celestial beings, living in another world, a world far removed from this world of mortal men? They live their life, we live ours, and we must live them to the full.'

The Epicurean assured his listeners that the gods cared nothing for their prayers, their sacrifices or their little sins; and that they should therefore try to find happiness and joy in this world, since it was the only world they had before they died and faded into nothingness.

Paul moved away and went to the next group, which was being addressed by a Stoic speaker.

'Listen to the inner voice of conscience,' the Stoic urged. 'That is the divine spark in each one of us, uniting us with that divine reason that created the world. Nothing matters but this: that we should live in harmony, following always the best in all things, taking no notice of the pain, the poverty or the injustice that may beset us. These things are not real; they have no part in the divine reason of which we are a part. You yourselves can become as gods, for the divine nature lives in you . . .'

As Paul listened to this philosophy which so resembled that of the Christians, his hopes rose. In his enthusiasm he suddenly called out, 'You are right, sir. The divine nature of the risen Christ!'

All heads turned to look at Paul. The speaker paused. This was just the kind of thing the people enjoyed: new ideas, argument, strangers bringing fresh topics for debate. A man near Paul questioned him: 'What did you say, stranger? Risen what?'

'Christ,' Paul explained. 'Jesus, the Son of God . . . Oh masters, you are so near to the truth. Your hearts and minds are open and prepared to receive the good news . . .'

The Stoic speaker was for the moment forgotten, as the crowd questioned Paul, asking what the good news was, and who was this risen Jesus. The Epicurean orator who had finished his discourse joined the Stoic, and good-humouredly asked who was the little man in black who had stolen his rival's audience.

The Stoic smiled and said he didn't mind losing his audience, as the man seemed to have something of interest to say. 'He looks like a Jew, but speaks like a Stoic,' he said. 'An interesting mixture, you must admit.'

A man standing near asked them to be quiet. He wanted to hear what Paul was saying.

'What *is* he saying?' asked the Stoic.

'Very like what you were saying,' was the answer, 'except that he professes a new god or gods. I caught the words "Jesus" and "resurrection".'

'Oh dear. *More* gods, and gods from the Orient at that!' laughed the Epicurean. 'He'd better be careful. This is the spot where the noble Socrates was made to drink hemlock for teaching the citizens that there were strange gods!'

But the Stoic was interested in what Paul was saying, and pushing his way with the Epicurean through the crowd, he got near him and asked him to explain to them the things which sounded strange to their ears, if they were matters of religion and philosophy.

It was the chance Paul had been praying for.

'You mean you wish me to address the people publicly?' he asked.

'If you will, from the steps,' said the Stoic, and led Paul to the Stoa Basilica, where all new preachers were heard. Paul stood under the painted arch, and looked at the crowd, which was bigger now and waiting silent and expectant. The Stoic asked his name, then turned to the people.

'Gentlemen,' he said, 'I present to you Paul of Tarsus, a

visitor to Athens who has something to tell us.'

He motioned Paul to step forward. He did so. Inwardly he was nervous and excited; outwardly he seemed calm and confident.

'Gentlemen of Athens,' he said, 'during my short stay in your beautiful city I have noticed one thing above all: that you are very religious, indeed very god-fearing. But among all the shrines and altars and statues, there was one in particular that seemed to me to express the searching that is behind your religion and your philosophies. It was a plain stone altar, and on it were inscribed the words "To the Unknown God". Friends, it is this "unknown" God whom I proclaim to you today, so that he may become known to you.'

He went on to say that there was only one God who was Lord of all, whether he was called divine reason or our Father. He had made human beings in his own image, and set in the hearts of men everywhere the desire to search for him and worship him.

'It is this desire,' he continued, 'implanted in us by God himself that makes men build temples and shrines and statues, but wouldn't we be foolish to suppose that the creator of the world can live in temples made by men?'

The time had come, he said, to put such foolish toys away and stretch upwards and outwards, to become a part of the great and glorious plan of God which he was going to tell them about.

'All down the ages,' he said, 'we have had glimpses of the Truth, but now God has given us the truth itself in a man who has become the living Truth. He is the one through whom we *know* what you have up to now called "The Unknown God". And so that everyone may know and believe that he and he only is the chosen one, God raised him from the dead and he is alive today . . .!'

Up to this moment the gathering had been listening intently. All Paul had said was in accordance with many of the ideas and beliefs they had heard from their own philosophers and religious teachers. When Paul led up to 'God's plan' they had been prepared for some new revelation, but the idea of a man raised from the dead reduced it to the ridiculous. Paul's fervent speech was interrupted by a shout of laughter. It was the last thing he had expected, and for him it was like a blow in the stomach. He stood dumb, the words frozen on his lips.

The people were as ready to mock now as they had been a moment before to listen. They broke into joking comment: 'We're to worship a dead man.' 'He's made fools of us. "Does he think we are children to be taken in with such a story?' 'Where is the man he says God sent?' 'Dead?' 'No, alive.' 'A walking corpse.'

Laughing, they began to disperse. Paul stood on the steps and watched them go, still frozen with shock. The Stoic was the last to leave. He put a kindly, rather condescending hand on Paul's shoulder, and said, 'Never mind. Personally I found your speech most interesting. I should like to hear more ... another day.'

He went on his way and Paul sank down on the steps, his head in his hands. He had failed.

8
Diana of
the Ephesians

AFTER Paul's bitter disappointment at his failure in Athens, he went to Corinth where he stayed with fellow tent-makers, Aquilla and his wife Priscilla. He kept in touch with Luke by letter, often using the willing Timothy as his scribe. Timothy and Silas had joined him there, bringing with them messages of faith and love from Luke and the young church in Philippi.

When he had spent three and a half years in Corinth, Paul decided that the time had come for him to revisit the churches in Asia and Syria. Priscilla and Aquilla travelled with him as far as Ephesus, the capital of Asia, where they were to stay and await Paul's return.

In Ephesus stood the temple of Diana, the goddess of fertility, worshipped all over the Roman province of Asia. Her great statue, believed to have fallen from heaven, stood at the entrance to the temple, and a good trade was done by the local silversmiths who sold replicas of the statue to residents and visitors.

Aquilla and Priscilla, a quiet, elderly couple whose homely manner might belie the fact that they were two of the most fearless and staunch of Paul's followers, carried on their work

of tent-making in this city. Each day they wondered how Paul
was faring and when he would return to them. But tonight they
were talking about someone else. Someone who had puzzled
and excited them.

'That young fellow, Apollos, who spoke in the synagogue—what do you make of him?' asked Priscilla, as she sat
weaving.

'Sounds to me,' answered her husband, 'as though he's
heard the story of Jesus somewhere and feels it his solemn duty
to spread it.'

They both agreed that the young man spoke from his heart,
and was a born orator like Paul, although he had never heard
of Paul or of the work of the churches.

'You should have asked him to come here to see us,' said
Priscilla.

'I did,' said her husband with a smile. 'He's coming today.'

Priscilla, protesting at not having been told, put aside her
work and bustled about fetching bread, wine and fruit.

'Wouldn't it be wonderful,' she said, 'if we could gather a
group of brethren, a church, in Ephesus to welcome Paul when
he comes back?'

'Well,' said her husband, mentioning two of the friends Paul
had made, 'Gaius and Aristarchus are here, and maybe
Timothy will come too.'

'I hope he does,' said Priscilla, checking over what she had
put on the table. 'I wish Paul had taken Timothy with him;
they're like father and son.'

There was a knock on the door, and Aquilla rose to open it.
On the threshold stood Apollos. He was a splendid-looking
young man, tall, strong and fearless. He brought a feeling of
youthful vigour into the little room, as he stepped into it.

'Welcome, my son. My wife, Priscilla. This is Apollos, my
dear, the young man we heard in the synagogue last sabbath.'

Priscilla made him welcome, and as she asked him to sit
down, and brought him a cup of wine, she told him how moved
she and Aquilla had been by the way he spoke—and of things
so close to their hearts.

Apollos took a sip of the wine. 'I spoke about Jesus of Nazareth,' he said, 'who I believe was Israel's Messiah.'

'Tell us, how did you come to hear of him?' asked Priscilla.

'Through some men who had been followers of someone called John the Baptist. Have you heard of him?'

'Oh yes,' said Aquilla at once. 'Yes indeed. We never met him, my wife and I, for we are natives of Italy and this is the farthest east we have ever been. But we have heard of John—you remember him, Priscilla: the man from Judea who foretold the coming of the Messiah.'

'And these men told you about Jesus?' Priscilla asked.

'No,' said Apollos. 'All they knew was that John had been arrested and then beheaded by Herod Antipas. They were still waiting for the Messiah to come.' Then he told them that when he had finished his studies at the university in Alexandria, he had decided to spend a year or two travelling, to see the world. He had never forgotten the story he had heard, and when he reached Judea he had tried to find out more. Then when he had nearly given up hope, he met two men in Jericho who were absolutely certain that the one John heralded had already come.

'Who were they?' asked Aquilla.

'One of them was a tax-collector, a smart business-like little man, named Zacchaeus; the other, his devoted friend who lived with him, was a man called Bartimeaus, as different from his friend as you could imagine. A big, rough-spoken fellow—told me he'd spent all his early life begging in the streets because he had been born blind.'

'Blind!' murmured Priscilla. 'Poor fellow.'

'But he wasn't blind when I met him,' Apollos continued, 'and that's how I learned the story of Jesus of Nazareth. It seems that just after John died news spread round Judea and Galilee of another, greater than John, who had the power to heal the sick and even to raise the dead. A man named Jesus. Bartimeaus had heard that blind men had had their sight restored by this Jesus, and when word reached Jericho that he and his disciples were coming through the town on their way to Jerusalem for the Passover, Bartimeaus took up a position at the gates and called out, "Son of David, have pity on me!" He believed that Jesus was the Messiah, you see.'

To his eager listeners he told the story of Bartimeaus's healing, and of how Jesus had said, 'Your faith has cured you'; how one moment he had been blind, and the next he saw the face of Jesus smiling at him.

There was a silence for a moment as all three marvelled at the miracle. Then Priscilla asked, 'And what about the other man?'

'Zacchaeus, the tax-collector? Jesus stayed with him at his house. It seems that Zacchaeus was hated in the town because he took advantage of his position to grow rich himself . . . If you met him now you couldn't believe that he had ever been like that. The house—and it is a big one—is open to everyone. Travellers, merchants, beggars, widows and orphans, the sick, the crippled and, of course, the blind can make their home there for as long as they like.'

'And it was Jesus that changed him?' asked Priscilla.

'Yes. He says he "saw the light" as much as Bartimeaus did. Says it was as though he had been lost before, lost among his own riches; sort of imprisoned by his own greed.'

'What did Jesus do?' asked Priscilla.

Apollos said that Zacchaeus didn't talk about it very much, but that he was just as certain as Bartimeaus. He had only told Apollos one thing that Jesus had said to him: 'This is what I came to do, to seek and to save the lost.'

Again his listeners were silent. The young man's eyes were shining. He was full of faith. He was indeed one of those of whom Jesus said, 'How happy are those who believe without seeing me!'

'That was all,' said Apollos at last. 'That was all I ever heard about him—except that he was dead. I couldn't believe that at first. It seemed to me that someone like that should never die.'

Priscilla and Aquilla looked at each other. They felt they must handle this precious gift of faith with care. Then Aquilla decided to lead Apollos to the truth step by step.

'And you have been preaching about him in the synagogues ever since?' he asked.

'I had to,' declared Apollos. 'It's become the most important thing in my life. You see, even though he's dead, even though he was cut off in the prime of his life—he was only thirty, you know—I'm sure that we can keep his name and his message alive. I think he would have wanted that to happen.'

'And what,' asked Aquilla, 'do you think his message was?'

'It was faith in God and his goodness. Love for our neighbours, even those who don't seem to merit it. And an utter disregard for our own welfare and safety, even to the point of death. That was the way he lived, and it's the way he meant us to live.'

'Apollos, my son,' said Aquilla, who was moved by what he had heard. 'God has sent you to us. You know so much of the truth, yet you are only at the beginning. First, know this. You are not alone in the work you have given your life to. All over Syria and Asia and in parts of Greece there are groups of people—churches we call them—dedicated to the service of Jesus.'

'But how . . .' asked Apollos in bewilderment.

'How did they hear him? Through his messengers: through those who knew him when he was alive, his disciples; and through those who have known him more recently.'

'What do you mean?' asked Apollos.

Aquilla sat beside him, and Priscilla drew nearer. There was an air of tense expectancy. Could they—a simple, faithful old couple—present their astonishing news in an acceptable way to the young man, or would they, like Paul in Athens, be laughed to silence?

Slowly and carefully Aquilla explained that Jesus was alive still, to those who had faith in him. Some had seen him, others had heard his voice, many felt his presence. He himself had never seen him, but had felt his presence many, many times. Indeed, at this moment he was very close.

'You mean his spirit—his ghost?' asked Apollos, puzzled.

'His Holy Spirit,' replied Aquilla, smiling, and continuing in his own homely way. 'His "Holy Ghost", if you like. But not a phantom from another world: a real, living spirit ready to pour itself into all men, to free them from their old sinful lives and unite them with the heavenly Father. This is what Jesus came to do, and he is still doing it—you told us just now in his own words . . .'

Apollos's face was filled with amazement and joy. He was not for one moment incredulous. It was as though he had found the missing link in his whole-hearted and reasoned faith.

'To seek and to save the lost,' he murmured.

That was the first of many meetings between the three of them—meetings at which Apollos learnt all that Aquilla and Priscilla could teach him. After he was baptized, it was decided that he should not stay in Ephesus, but should go to join Timothy in Corinth. Once he was established there, this would free Timothy to come to Ephesus where, to the great joy of Aquilla and Priscilla, Paul had returned and was preaching in a great hall called the 'Gymnasium of Tyrannus' each day from eleven in the morning until four. Every day these meetings were filled with those who were ill and the cripples, and with people bringing the clothing and handkerchiefs of their bedridden friends for Paul to bless. He had worked many miracles of healing, and his teaching had caused a number of Ephesian sorcerers to pile their books together in the market-place and burn them publicly. This had created a very great stir in the city.

But the success of Paul's mission in Ephesus had a very disturbing effect on one group of people. Since those who became followers of Jesus no longer bought images of the goddess Diana, sales had fallen considerably, and the silversmiths were uneasy. Their leader and spokesman, Demetrius, a fiery, eloquent man with the welfare of his fellow-workers very much at heart, saw their living threatened and called a meeting in his work-shop.

'Comrades,' he said, 'many of you know why this meeting has been called. Like me, you are all skilled workers in silver, and like me you are all faithful servants of the great goddess, Diana of the Ephesians, upon whom we depend for our living.'

There was a rumble of assent, and a mumbling of 'Great is Diana of the Ephesians'. Demetrius began to warm to his subject. He told them that their livelihood was threatened by a foreigner who was spreading lies. They must have heard of him, and of his pernicious teaching.

'Paul is out to destroy,' he said, 'and we, the workers, must unite together and stop him before we find our living taken away from us and our wives and children begging for bread.'

An elderly craftsman interrupted. 'What's he done, Demetrius? I haven't heard of him.'

'I'll tell you what he's done,' said Demetrius. 'He's gone around saying that gods made by hand are not gods at all. Told the people that it is wrong to worship them—declared that they have no power.'

One or two listeners laughed, but others who had done poor business with their souvenirs turned on them in protest. Demetrius drove home his point with a practical example. He showed them the tray of statuettes, and said that last year they would have been sold out in a week, with him working twelve hours a day to keep up with the demand of pilgrims to the temple. Now, half his stock was left in his hands.

Others told of similar trade losses, and those who feared Demetrius's power made up tales, and murmured that the bread was being taken out of their mouths. Demetrius stirred them to action when he reminded them that this month was the Feast of Diana, when the city would be filled with foreign visitors. They relied on these festival weeks for most of their sales. Were they to see those sales ruined by a dangerous madman?

'He's got power,' he said. 'He's got some sort of influence over people. Else why have they stopped buying the images? And why did those men—doctors, astrologers—burn their books?'

Since no one answered him, he told them the value of those books: 50,000 drachmas gone up in smoke, more money than any of them would see in five years. A man who could make sensible people burn good money could only be—and he paused to let the words sink in—an enemy of the people.

'If we let this enemy of the people get away with his lies and his sorcery, you know the next thing that'll happen, don't you? He'll set out to destroy the temple itself.'

There were angry cries now from his listeners—except for one old man, who maintained that Paul wouldn't have power to do much harm.

At that, Demetrius got well into his stride. There were hundreds of these people, and not only Jews, in the city and all over Asia—their numbers growing every day. As for power, what was it made them able to make cripples walk, blind men see, scholars burn their books, religious men turn from the worship of their gods, if it was not a wicked, and evil power?

Such was his eloquence that his fellow-craftsmen believed all that he said: that by taking steps against Paul, they were defending their religion and their very lives. 'Let us go forward as one man,' urged Demetrius, 'crying with one voice "Great is Diana of the Ephesians".'

In Aquilla and Priscilla's lodgings everything was peaceful. Aquilla and Paul were examining bundles of goat's hair which they lifted from a cupboard in the corner of the room. They brought it to the work bench to sort it out, now and then handing strands to Priscilla who was spinning the thread which would be woven into tent material.

'It's a poor quality wool, this,' said Paul. 'Not as good as the stuff you had in Corinth.'

'I know,' Aquilla told him. 'I've tried everywhere to get imported goat's hair, but there's not much sale for it, it seems.'

'Tarsus was the place,' said Paul. 'Those long-haired goats from the Taurus mountains, you know . . . wonderful cloth. The best in the world.'

Aquilla pointed out that none the less they had done good trade in these last weeks with the festival pilgrims—since it was so hard to get lodgings they had been glad of a tent whatever the quality.

They were busy sorting, and Priscilla protested that Paul

should not be working, but resting. He was preaching five hours a day, and that was enough.

Paul laughed. 'If a man doesn't work he doesn't eat!'

'There's plenty to eat without you having to work day and night,' she retorted.

'Dear Priscilla—you're like a mother to me,' said Paul.

They went on quietly working, too busy to talk much, when from the distance they heard shouting. Soon they could distinguish the words, repeated over and over again: 'Great is Diana of the Ephesians'. Then they heard footsteps running down the street. The door burst open, and their two friends, Gaius and Aristarchus, burst into the room.

'Paul,' said Aristarchus breathlessly. 'Run and hide . . . There's rioting in the streets . . . a mob is on its way here.'

'Rioting? What about?' Paul demanded.

Gaius told them to listen, and they heard the shouting coming nearer. Aquilla spoke calmly, assuring them that they often called out 'Great is Diana of the Ephesians' at festival time; but Aristarchus interrupted him, with urgency in his voice.

'No,' he said, 'it's more than that. The silversmiths are up in arms against Paul and his teaching. With Demetrius as leader they've managed to stir the crowds to a frenzy. They're in a dangerous mood.'

Paul went on working. 'I'm used to danger,' he said. 'Let them come and we'll see what it's all about.'

'I can tell you what it's about,' said Aristarchus. 'They're demanding that you should be brought to the amphitheatre to face the charges.'

'What charges?' asked Paul.

'Sacrilege against the goddess Diana,' said Gaius. 'Paul, hide yourself.'

Paul said, unmoved, that he could face their charges, but as the shouting came nearer Priscilla forced him to listen to her. She said the churches were in Paul's hands—no one could carry on his work. Any of them could be spared, but not him. She spoke with great authority, ignoring his protests; and with Aquilla's help she pushed Paul towards the store of goat's hair, and piled the wool over him till he was completely hidden—but not before she had snatched his round skull cap from his head. She threw it to Gaius, begging him in an urgent whisper to put it on and go with Aquilla to the work bench.

Outside Demetrius hammered on the door. In a matter of seconds Priscilla was at her spinning-wheel, Paul was crouched underneath the wool, and Gaius and Aquilla were at the bench, working. Aristarchus, at a nod from Priscilla, threw open the door. There stood Demetrius flanked by two of the toughest silversmiths, and behind them the mob still chanting, 'Great is Diana of the Ephesians.'

'There he is!' shouted Demetrius, pointing at Gaius.

'What do you want?' asked Aristarchus, to which Demetrius replied, 'Paul of Tarsus.'

Gaius rose. 'What can I do for you?' he asked.

Demetrius stared at him. 'You can come with us to the amphitheatre, then you'll see.'

Aquilla tried to gain time. 'This is my house,' he said. 'You must tell me who you are and what this intrusion means.'

'We are honest workmen who see our living being snatched from us by that viper there!' said Demetrius. Aquilla replied quietly that they too were honest workmen who had done nothing to hurt anyone.

Demetrius brushed him aside. 'Keep quiet, old man, if you value your life.' Pointing at Gaius he said to his companion, 'Seize him. Take him to the amphitheatre.'

Aquilla and Priscilla tried to stand in front of Gaius to protect him, but the two silversmiths pushed them roughly aside and grabbed hold of him, hustling him towards the door. Aristarchus made a vain effort to shut the door and prevent their going; but more of the silversmiths had gathered there and pushed it back. Demetrius ordered him out of the way.

'What are you going to do with him?' demanded Aristarchus.

'Throw him to the beasts!' said one of the silversmiths, and the cry was taken up by the others outside the door. Aquilla and Priscilla looked anxiously towards the cupboard where Paul was hidden, certain that hearing this he would come out and tell them who he was. With great presence of mind Priscilla swayed as if she were fainting, and Aquilla laid her down across the store cupboard, blocking the way. Demetrius whipped round suspiciously, but Aristarchus, realizing that the silversmiths must be got out of the house immediately if Paul was to be saved, made a sudden lunge at the men in the doorway. In a moment he was struggling with two of the silversmiths, and Demetrius's attention was taken from everything else.

'Seize that one too and take him along,' shouted Demetrius.

With more hysterical shouts the mob dragged Gaius and Aristarchus through the door and down the street.

There was silence in the room, broken by a moan from Priscilla. 'God be with them,' she cried. 'Oh, dear Jesus, stay near them.'

Aquilla helped her to her feet, while Paul struggled out from his hiding place. For once he stood helpless.

'What have we done?' he asked in despair. 'What have we sent them to? Dear God, why should men risk their lives for me?'

The mob poured down the street, growing larger as it went, until the uproar was deafening. Every man yelled some slogan, and the air was hideous with cries of 'Throw them to the lions', 'Kill them . . .' 'Down with the Jews . . .' Workers of Ephesus, unite . . .' 'Burn the heretics . . .' 'Let the beasts get at them . . .' 'Demetrius, Demetrius, we want Demetrius . . .' But one cry was loudest of all: 'Great is Diana of the Ephesians.'

Buffeted and bleeding, Gaius and Aristarchus were pushed through the angry crowd. Workmen, crazy with excitement, shook their fists and yelled at them.

On they went till they reached the amphitheatre, and there they lifted Demetrius shoulder high, and carried him, flushed and triumphant, past the dens where the hungry lions paced restlessly up and down behind the bars.

On the fringe of the mob a group of Jews, caught up

unwillingly in the crowd, tried to make their way out of the amphitheatre, but found their path barred by some of the workmen who yelled out that here were more of them—more Jews to be thrown to the lions.

Terrified, one of the Jews pleaded with them: 'I'm one of you. I am a coppersmith. You know me. I'm Alexander the coppersmith!'

They were saved by the arrival of the town clerk, a popular man, who broke up the struggling mass of silversmiths and Jews with a brisk, 'Order . . . Order! What's all this about?'

While the Jew was hysterically explaining that he was Alexander the coppersmith, the workmen all spoke at once, saying that he was a Jew who would spit at the temple of Diana, and that all Jews should be thrown to the lions.

The town clerk gave some terse orders. 'Get back and pull yourselves together,' he said to the workmen, and to Alexander, 'You get off home, Alexander, and warn all Jews to keep away.'

The Jew hurried off thankfully, and the town clerk turned again to the workmen.

'Now then,' he said, 'what's all this about and who started it?'

One of the silversmiths answered him: 'Demetrius the silversmith, sir, he's over there. It's all in order, sir; the Jews have been desecrating the temple, destroying our images, sir, burning our books, sir, practising black magic, sir. Demetrius has got the ringleaders, sir, in chains, sir, over there, sir . . .'

'That's enough,' the town clerk stopped him curtly. 'Take me to him. We'll see if it's "All in order, sir".'

He strode purposefully through the crowd to where Demetrius was now standing on a dais. Gaius and Aristarchus, chained together, stood beside him. Demetrius was exhibiting them amid cheering, and cries of 'Demetrius', 'Demetrius'.

The town clerk mounted the dais. 'Call them to order, Demetrius,' he said.

Demetrius was suddenly embarrassed. 'Why it's you, sir. Look, we've captured two dangerous criminals, sir.'

'We'll see about that,' said the town clerk. 'Now, quieten this mob.'

Demetrius recognized authority when he saw it. He held up his arms and addressed the people.

'Quiet! Quiet! Order for his excellency the town clerk.'

The cheering and the shouts died down and were replaced by expectant murmurs. Then there was silence, and the town clerk stepped forward.

'Gentlemen of Ephesus,' he said, 'I think you must have worn yourselves out with your shouting. You have certainly nearly deafened me.'

He was greeted with laughter, and when that had died down, he said that the city had rung for more than two hours with their cry of 'Great is Diana of the Ephesians,' and all to no purpose, since it did not need their shouts to remind men of that unquestioned fact. They had been working themselves up to a pitch of wild and rash behaviour, and he advised them to calm themselves before they did anything which they would afterwards regret.

He turned to Demetrius. 'Now, what is your quarrel with these two men?'

'They intend to desecrate the temple,' said Demetrius, without hesitation.

The town clerk asked Gaius and Aristarchus if this was true. They denied it. He then asked Demetrius if he had seen them desecrate the temple or heard them abuse the goddess Diana.

Demetrius was beginning to be ill at ease. 'No but . . .'

'You have brought these men here by force,' said the town clerk. 'This in itself is against the law.' He turned again to the crowd. 'You have no just charge against these men. On Demetrius's own admission, they have neither robbed the temple nor used blasphemous language against our goddess.'

He was interrupted by a surly shout of 'They've taken our trade away, how about that?' and some angry mutterings; but he continued sternly, 'If Demetrius and his fellow craftsmen have a complaint against these men and wish to bring a charge against them, the courts are open and there are magistrates. Let them take legal action. If there is any matter outside the jurisdiction of the magistrates' court, then it must be settled in the regular assembly. I tell you, you yourselves stand in danger of being charged with rioting after today's events. There is no excuse whatsoever for this disorderly behaviour. Now, go home quietly.'

He ordered Demetrius to take the chains off Gaius and Aristarchus. When they were free he apologized to them for the disturbance, but advised them in future to keep their opinions to themselves.

He strode off without a backward look. Demetrius watched him go, then spat contemptuously at his former prisoners, and lumbered off, grumbling, with his comrades. Gaius and Aristarchus looked at each other, and weakly smiled their relief at their escape as they rubbed the sore places made by the chains on their wrists.

After the uproar in Ephesus had died down, Paul gathered together all the believers in the city and renewed their enthusiasm with his words of hope and encouragement. Then, taking with him Gaius and Aristarchus, friends to whom he owed so much, he crossed over once more to Macedonia.

There was great rejoicing at the house of Lydia when Paul returned to Philippi. Luke in particular was thankful to see him safe and well. Once again he met the prison governor and his family, and was introduced to the many new members of the growing church.

But he was anxious to go to Corinth, where he and Luke learned to their distress that the brethren were beginning to divide themselves into separate groups. Apollos had been doing great work there, but if anything he was too attractive and eloquent a speaker. He himself said that it might be his way of teaching that had encouraged the people to split up and have favourite preachers, calling themselves 'Paul's men' or 'Apollos's men'.

Paul made short work of this misguided spirit, saying, 'Who was it died on the cross for you? Was it Paul or Apollos? No, it was Christ alone. We who speak to you are servants of the one

Lord. It is not fine words that should move your hearts, but the gospel of truth that you share one with another. The gospel of Christ.'

Three months later, more journeys were planned. Paul and Luke stood by the quayside waving farewell to Timothy, Gaius and Aristarchus who had set sail for Troas, where they proposed to wait for Paul and Luke at the inn of their old friend Carpus. Then Paul and Luke returned to Philippi to celebrate the Passover.

When they finally reached Troas, it was only for a week's stay. On the Friday night they were to have a meeting in the room at the inn where Paul and Luke had first met. There Carpus, the innkeeper, was lighting lamps and candles and setting out bread and wine, helped by his young son, Eutychus, who was urging his father to let him stay up not only for the meal but for the meeting afterwards. He had never heard Paul speak. 'This may be the last chance,' he pleaded. 'Timothy says he's leaving tomorrow.'

'Always on the move, Paul is', said his father. 'He's not been here more than a week. Well, I'm glad that doctor, Luke, is with him. He needs taking care of, and that's a fact. Where's he off to this time, Timothy?'

He was off to Jerusalem, Timothy explained, to celebrate the Feast of Pentecost, having missed getting there for the Passover. He had been all ready to sail when they were in Corinth when it was learnt that some of his fellow passengers, Jews, were plotting to do away with him on the voyage. His friends managed to persuade him not to risk it.

'You mean they would have murdered him?' asked Eutychus.

'That's it, Eutychus. Oh, it wouldn't be the first attempt on his life. He's pretty used to it by now.'

And there would be more, said Carpus, and added gloomily that he thought Paul would never reach Jerusalem—all that way with people plotting against him at every stage of the journey. 'He's not too popular in Jerusalem,' he went on, 'or so I hear. Whatever does he want to go there at all for?'

Timothy reminded him of what he had forgotten: that Paul was still a Jew, and that this day was in fact the Jewish sabbath, and that the meal and the service were all part of the Jewish way of life.

'I know,' said Carpus. 'And I don't deny that they've done a lot for us poor sinners. To show us the way, I mean. The Son of God wouldn't have chosen to be born a Jew for no reason. But if you ask me, they've lost their chance. They're so tied up in all the old teaching that they don't know the truth when they see it . . . I know you're part Jew yourself, lad, and I mean no offence, but it worries me no end to see our Paul putting his head into the lion's mouth, as it were.'

Timothy laughed at his fears. 'Oh, I don't think it'll be as bad as that. It isn't only for Pentecost that he's going. He's missed many of those before now. But he's got to keep in touch with the brethren in Jerusalem the same as everywhere else. There's terrible poverty among them, you know, and Paul's made a collection for them from the brethren in Greece.'

They were still talking, and Eutychus had been given permission to stay up, when Paul and Luke came in, with Gaius and Aristarchus. Paul congratulated Carpus on having borrowed so many lamps for the feast—so many that they made the room hot. Eutychus, glad to be of use, opened the window, and stood looking down on the courtyard below. 'There's quite a crowd waiting down there,' he said. 'Can I tell them to come up?' And having got permission, he leaned out and called to the people below to come up to the third floor.

When they were all gathered in the room above, they sang a psalm, and the meal was eaten. The service that followed it went on far into the night. The tall, new candles in the branched candlestick had burned to almost nothing, and still the people listened, spellbound, to the voice of Paul.

He spoke to them of spiritual gifts, of the Holy Spirit working in men. 'God works through different men in different ways,' he said. 'As a human body is one body and yet has many parts, so it is with the body of Christ of which we are all members. For that is what the church is. The body of Christ.

Now, as we know, a body is not one single organ. It is composed of many organs, many limbs. If the foot should say, "Because I am not a hand, I don't belong to the body", it would not alter the fact, would it, that the foot *is* part of the body? If the ear should say, "I can't see, therefore I can't be part of the body", does this make the ear any less useful?' There was a ripple of laughter from his listeners, and when it had died down Paul went on to say that as God had given each part of the body its own function, making together a harmonious whole, so in the body of Christ, his church on earth, they would find the same principles of harmony.

'Through the grace of God we have different gifts. It is up to us to use them to the very best of our ability. Pray at all times and be ready to receive the greatest gifts of the Spirit. And pray most of all for the gift of love. For I may be able to speak the languages of men and even of angels, but if I have no love, my speech is no more than a noisy gong or a clanging bell. I may have the gift of inspired preaching; I may have all knowledge and understand all secrets; I may have all the faith needed to move mountains—but if I have no love, I am nothing. I may give away everything I have, and even give up my body to be burnt—but if I have no love, this does me no good. Love is patient and kind; it is not jealous or conceited or proud; love is not ill-mannered or selfish or irritable; love does not keep a record of wrongs; love is not happy with evil, but is happy with the truth. Love never gives up; and its faith, hope, patience never fail. Love is eternal.

'There are inspired messages, but they are temporary; there is knowledge but it will pass. For our gifts of knowledge and of inspired messages are only partial; but when what is perfect comes, then what is partial will disappear. What we see now is like a dim image in a mirror; then we shall see face to face. Meanwhile these three remain: faith, hope, and love; and the greatest of these is love.'

Eutychus had tried hard to keep awake, to hear every word that Paul said. He sat on the ledge of the open window, his back against the closed shutter, his head nodding, until by the end of the speech he was fast asleep, oblivious to the rustle of comment among the people in the room who had been deeply moved by Paul's address.

As Paul sat down, Luke asked Carpus to bless the bread and the wine. He took a loaf of bread in his hands and Timothy prompted him in the Hebrew blessing: 'Thanks be to you, God, King of the universe, who brings forth bread from the earth.'

Carpus broke the bread and handed the halves to the people on his right and left. As he reached for the jug of wine, Eutychus, sound asleep, slipped sideways against the shutter. It flew open under his weight and with nothing to stop him he fell out, over the sill and down into the courtyard three floors below.

A woman screamed, 'It's Eutychus; he's fallen!' Carpus with a cry of horror rushed to the window.

The boy's body lay on the paving of the courtyard way below. Carpus turned and rushed to the door. Luke seized a lamp, and with Paul and Timothy hurried after him.

They raced down the stairs into the courtyard, where Carpus dropped to his knees beside the boy, and held him in his arms. The boy's head dropped backwards. With great gulping sobs Carpus held him to him, and then at last looked up at Luke who held the light which shone down on the boy.

'Do something for him, doctor,' pleaded Carpus through his tears. 'You can, can't you?'

Luke put his hand on his shoulder to steady him and told him to take the lamp.

Very gently Carpus lowered the boy to the ground again and tremblingly got to his feet. He took the lamp from Luke who knelt beside Eutychus and felt his heart. Carpus thought he saw the doctor shake his head and his fear changed to certainty as Timothy and Luke lifted the limp body of his son and laid him on a bench. Suddenly he was aware of Paul standing beside him and of Paul's voice, 'Don't be afraid.' He watched, scarcely daring to hope, as Paul sat on the bench beside the still figure and took the boy's head in his hands.

In the room above the men and women were crowded at the

window. The women, certain that the boy must be dead after such a fall, were already wailing. They saw Paul leave the lamplit group and cross the courtyard towards the house. All eyes turned towards the door as they heard his footsteps coming up the stairs. The women were still wailing as he entered the room.

'There's no need to mourn,' he said briskly. 'The lad is alive.' And then, before they could question him, he pointed to the deserted table. 'Come,' he said. 'The bread and wine are waiting.'

As the people gathered round the table again, Paul picked up the bread, and said, 'My brothers, this supper that we eat together is the Lord's supper. We eat the bread and drink the wine as members of one body of which Christ is the head, remembering as we do so the last supper that he ate with his disciples on the night that he was betrayed. On that night he took the bread, and after giving thanks he broke it, and said, "Take and eat. This is my body which is broken for you. Do this in remembrance of me".'

He broke the bread and handed it to the people on his right and left hand, who in turn broke it and handed a piece on to their neighbours. Paul took the jug of wine and poured it into a cup.

'In the same way, after supper, he took the cup saying, "This cup means the new covenant in my blood. Whenever you drink from it remember me".'

Paul drank from the cup, then passed it to the neighbour on his left. It was passed round from hand to hand, each drinking from it. And suddenly a sound at the door made them all turn to look. There, with Carpus and Luke on either side of him, was Eutychus, a little stunned by what had happened, but alive and well. A place was made for the boy at the table, and Gaius broke a piece of bread and gave it to him, while someone held the cup for him on the other side.

Eutychus looked across the table at Paul, and Paul smiled at him and said, 'Eat and drink, my son. And the body of our Lord Jesus Christ which was given for you, preserve your body and soul to everlasting life.'

9
Jerusalem

FROM Troas Paul began the long journey to Jerusalem. Feeling the need for a day on his own, he set out on foot while Luke and his other friends boarded a ship sailing to Assos where Paul joined them. They sailed past the islands of Mitylene, Chios and Samos, and since the ship had to wait off Miletus to load cargo, Paul had asked the elders of the church at Ephesus to meet him there so that he might say farewell to them. Paul and Luke were taken ashore in a rowing-boat, and landed in the midst of a busy scene as the local people loaded their boats with bales and bundles to be taken to the ship, which was anchored some way out.

Waiting on the beach to greet them were the brethren from Ephesus. After the greetings Paul, his back to the sea, oblivious to the shouts of the men loading the boats, spoke to his friends.

'My brothers,' he said, 'I am going to Jerusalem, and although I do not know what will happen to me there, the Holy Spirit has made it plain to me that in every town I visit there will be trouble and persecution. I do not care about that. I count my life as nothing compared with the joy of finishing the course I run, which is to complete the task the Lord Jesus gave me in preaching the good news of God's grace. But I know that not one of you will ever see me again, and so keep watch over yourselves, and over your flock. For you are the shepherds and I know well that ravening wolves will come among you when I am gone. Yes, there will be those among you who will pervert the truth and find disciples to follow them. Be on your guard therefore and remember how for three whole years I myself was with you night and day, caring for you and warning you, often with tears. Now I entrust you to God, who in his grace can strengthen you to take your place among his saints.'

The little group knelt down on the beach, and as Paul stretched out his hands over them in blessing, he remembered a last word of advice.

'You remember,' he said, 'how these hands of mine have always provided enough for my needs and for my companions. I have tried to show you that it is our duty to work hard so that we can help the poor, remembering the words of the Lord Jesus who said, "It is better to give than to receive".'

Then he knelt down on the beach among them, praying: 'O God, Father of Our Lord Jesus Christ and Father of all men everywhere. Strengthen us, we beg you, and fill us with the grace of your Holy Spirit, so that our lives will be founded on the love which passes human understanding. To you, O God, who by your power within us can do anything, may the church bring glory to you through Christ Jesus.'

Tears fell as Paul rose to his feet and embraced each one of them. Then he and Luke turned back to the edge of the sea, where the rowing-boat was waiting for them. They climbed in, the boat was pushed out, and once again they boarded the ship which was to take them to Cæsarea. From there they travelled by land to Jerusalem for the Feast of Pentecost.

It was twenty-three years since that other day of Pentecost when the story of the acts of Christ's apostles began.

They were going first to see James 'The Just' who was now the leader of the church in Jerusalem. He welcomed them glad-ly and Paul handed him the money he had collected through Greece and Asia to help in the work of the church. Then he introduced him to Luke, who noticed a certain embarrassment in James's greeting. There was still strong feeling among some of the Christian Jews against Paul's wholehearted acceptance of the Gentiles.

After they had been in the city for seven days, Paul and four of the brethren went to the temple sanctuary for a particular ceremony. It was all familiar to Paul: the speakers at Solomon's Porch, the beggars at the Beautiful Gate, the groups of pupils listening to the rabbis; but to Luke it was new, and while he waited for Paul and the others in the Court of the Gentiles, he listened to one particular rabbi, a fine, vigorous-looking old man who sat with about a dozen young men in a circle at his feet, listening intently to the words he read.

'When the day comes for the new covenant, said the Lord, I will set my laws within men's *minds* and write them on their *hearts*. I will be their God and they will be my people. One citizen will no longer teach his fellows to know the Lord, for all will know me, from the least to the greatest. And I will be merciful to them and I will no longer remember their sins . . .'

Paul had come from the gate leading into the sanctuary, and as he stood beside Luke, listening with him to the old rabbi, the years seemed to fall away and he imagined himself as one of the rapt young men in the class.

The old man had reached the end of his lesson. He rolled up the scroll and dismissed his pupils, saying, 'Meditate on these words tonight, my sons, and tomorrow when you come we will discuss their meaning.'

The young men began to rise to their feet. The rabbi became aware of Paul and Luke, and glanced inquiringly towards them. Paul stepped forward.

'Rabbi Gamaliel,' he said, 'I am happy to see you well after so many years.' Then, seeing the old man looking puzzled, he went on, 'Do you remember a pupil of yours, it must be—oh, twenty-three years ago. A young man called Saul of Tarsus?'

'Saul of Tarsus,' echoed Gamaliel, looking searchingly at Paul. 'Why yes . . . There was some trouble, if I remember. Where have you been all these years, my son?'

'Travelling.'

'And now you're back among your people. Who is this?' he asked, suddenly noticing Luke.

When Paul told him that this was his friend, Luke, from Macedonia, the old man was taken aback for an instant to think that his former pupil was in the company of a Gentile. His greeting was civil, but cold.

He turned back to Paul with some relief, and asked more about his travels. They talked on, unaware that they were being watched in an unfriendly manner by a group of men nearby. In the centre of the group, and obviously the most emphatic personality among them, was the merchant from Iconium, who had come to Jerusalem as one of the Pentecost pilgrims. With him was the Jewish baker from Lystra who had warned Timothy.

'There he is again,' said the merchant. 'I told you we'd find him here. And look . . . he has a Gentile with him. Doesn't that prove what I've been telling you? He's been desecrating the sanctuary by taking Greeks in there.'

'He does not care about the Law at all,' said the baker, remembering his last encounter with Paul.

'That's right,' said the merchant. 'That's what I've been telling them. All over Asia he's been perverting Jews from the law of Moses. We had trouble with him in Galatia, years ago. Had him run out of the city, we did, in our town. But in other places he managed to get quite a following, I'm told.'

A local Jew, rigid in his observance of Jewish law, was more fierce in his disapproval. 'Who cares what followers he has among the Gentiles?' he said. 'Let him perish in ignorance with them! But to desecrate the temple! To take heathens into the house of God!' With his arms above his head he turned to the crowd. 'Children of Abraham, do you hear? The house of God is desecrated.'

A wail went up from the older men, angry shouts from the younger ones. The merchant was well satisfied. He had roused them against Paul, and now he reminded them that he need not tell them their business for they were well aware that breaking the temple laws might be punished with death.

'Yes,' he asserted. 'And death for whom? Not for the stupid pagan who follows like a sheep into the sanctuary, but for'—he raised his voice to a shout—'Paul of Tarsus!'

The crowd, now thoroughly roused, took up the cry: 'Death to Paul of Tarsus. Death to Paul of Tarsus!' They surged forward—the devout pilgrims to the Feast of Pentecost had become an ugly mob.

Just too late to stop them a Roman soldier who had heard the shouting hurried down the steps that led from the Tower of Antonia into the court. For a moment he watched the disorderly scene, then realizing that he alone could do nothing, he ran back up the steps into the tower for reinforcements.

In his room the commander, Claudius Lysias, was watching a couple of orderlies polishing his breastplate and helmet, when a soldier came in in some haste to report that there was trouble down below, in the temple courtyard.

'What do you mean, trouble?' demanded Claudius Lysias.

The soldier told him that a mob of Jews was setting on a couple of men, and that it looked ugly.

'Oh, these Jews,' said the commander. 'If it isn't Pentecost it's the Passover, and always a disturbance. But they usually keep it out of the holy temple. And we're short of men in barracks today—they're posted all through the city.'

He turned to the two orderlies, telling them they would have to go. They helped him on with his breastplate and then hurried out with the other soldier. Claudius Lysias went to the door and looked down the barracks steps. He saw the three soldiers pushing their way through the crowd and the guards from the Beautiful Gate making their way from the other side of the courtyard. In the centre of the yelling mob stood Paul, buffeted on every side by angry people, until the soldiers reached him and tried to force the crowd back. But they could not control the surging mob.

Claudius Lysias saw that he must act quickly. He hurried down the steps, and roared, 'Stand back!'

The crowd recognized the voice of authority. They drew

back, and when they saw the commander made way for him. He marched through them, to the heart of the trouble. In his curt, military voice he asked Paul who he was, and what was happening, but before Paul could answer the crowd began shouting again.

'He has desecrated the temple!' 'He's a blasphemer!' 'He practises sorcery!' 'Crucify him!'

'Bring him to the barracks,' Claudius Lysias ordered the soldiers. 'Better carry him.'

Four soldiers hoisted Paul above their heads, and the commander led the way back to the barracks. The mob went with them, angry hands clutching up at Paul and making it difficult for the soldiers to make any progress. They struggled up the steps at last, and put him down at the top. There Paul asked for permission to speak.

'I am a Jew,' he said, 'a man from Tarsus. I have done nothing which is against the Law.'

'They seem to think you have,' said the commander; and Paul asked if he could speak to the crowd.

'Speak to them?' echoed Claudius Lysias. 'Don't you realize they tried to murder you?'

But Paul insisted, and the commander, curious, said he might try. Paul turned to the crowd below and held out his arms.

'My brothers and fathers,' he said, 'listen to what I have to say in my defence.'

It was the Hebrew form of address, and it immediately silenced them.

Paul told them that he was a Jew, as they were, that he was born in Tarsus of Cilicia, but had been brought up here in Jerusalem guided by the most honoured Rabbi Gamaliel, and trained in the strictest observance of the Jewish law to be zealous for God. He reminded them that it was he who had persecuted the men and women who were followers of Jesus the Nazarene, and that it was with the authority of the high priest and the council that he went to Damascus to bring the Nazarenes in chains to Jerusalem.

'My brethren and fathers,' he went on, 'it was on the road to Damascus that the thing happened to me that changed my life.' He paused, and the crowd waited in silence. 'I had nearly reached the city, in fact I could see the gates just ahead of me, when suddenly I was stopped in my tracks by a blinding, blazing light. In terror, I fell to the ground, and as I lay there I heard a voice calling my name: "Saul . . . Saul"; and as I listened, not daring to speak, the voice said, "Why do you persecute me?" Still trembling with fear, I looked up into the light, asking to know who it was that spoke, and the voice said, "I am Jesus of Nazareth, the one you persecute".'

There was absolute silence in the courtyard. The crowd was hushed, spellbound by Paul's story.

'My companions ran up to me,' he went on. 'They found me staring up into the light with sightless eyes. I had been blinded by the glory of that vision, and as a blind man Saul the persecutor was led into Damascus. Would you not say that it was the hand of the Lord that struck me blind? Hear then what happened in Damascus, and see the hand of the Lord again at work upon me. A devout Jew, a reverent observer of the law, a man highly respected by all the Jews in Damascus, came to me as I lay blind in my lodgings and put his hands on my eyes, and through the power of the Lord the sight was restored to them. This man, Ananias, told me: "The God of our fathers has chosen you to know his will, to see the Messiah, to hear words from his own lips that you may be his witness to all men".'

The crowd was still listening intently. It seemed as though he had won them over. Everything he had said so far had had the ring of truth to their ears. Encouraged, he continued.

'Soon after this I returned to Jerusalem so that I might bear witness to the Messiah here in the very place where I had watched his first martyr, Stephen, stoned to death. But again the Lord intervened. He told me to leave this city and . . . I will tell you the Lord's own words . . . "Go," he said. "For I will send you far away to carry my name to the Gentiles".'

At this last word frenzy broke out again in the crowd.

'Away with him!' one screamed, and others, 'He is condemned by his own words!' 'He has turned to the Gentiles!', 'He is a traitor, he should die!'

And the crowd, easily swayed, first muttered and then joined in the insistent clamour: 'Away with him . . . Death to the traitor . . .'

The pandemonium was worse now than before. Claudius Lysias listened with exasperation. He had not made head or tail of Paul's speech, nor of the explosive behaviour of this Hebrew mob. He turned angrily to Paul, told him curtly he had had his say, and much good had it done him.

Paul was bitterly disappointed. 'They don't understand . . .' he murmured; and Claudius Lysias said briskly that he didn't understand either, and that Paul had better tell him what he had done.

'I have done nothing against the Law,' said Paul firmly, and at that the commander ordered the soliders to take him inside.

'To be flogged, sir?' asked one of the soldiers.

'Yes. We've got to make him talk.'

Two of the soldiers hustled Paul into the barracks, while the commander ordered the others to clear the courtyard. He watched the mob disperse, then went inside and into his room, where stood Paul between the two soldiers, his hands bound in front of him. His coat had been stripped off.

'Why is he here?' asked Claudius Lysias. 'I thought I told you to examine him under the lash.'

'Yes, sir,' said one of the soldiers. 'But the prisoner says he's a Roman citizen, sir. And it's against orders . . .'

Claudius Lysias was startled. He asked Paul sternly if he realized that the penalty for making a false claim to Roman citizenship was death. Paul said he did. But he still insisted that he was a Roman citizen.

The commander looked at him keenly and put a test question. 'What did it cost you?' he asked.

'Nothing,' said Paul. 'I was born a citizen.'

Immediately, the soldiers were ordered to release him and to unbind his hands. The commander apologized for what had happened; but he went on, 'I can't just let you go, you know.

The Jews are making accusations against you, though I can't make head or tail what they are. You'll have to stand some sort of a trial, if only for your own safety.'

Paul replied that he could answer any charge that might be brought against him to which the commander said that he would order the council of the Sanhedrin to meet, and that on the next day Paul could face them and defend himself.

In the council chamber the Sanhedrin met on the next day with its usual ceremony. In the judge's chair sat Ananias, the high priest, and next to him were representatives of the Sadducees. Opposite sat the Pharisees, among them old Gamaliel with his pupils, and in the centre stood Paul, as Stephen had at his trial so long ago. Only the high priest seemed an unfamiliar figure, very different from his clever and scholarly predecessor. Ananias was a gross, worldly man, with a reputation for violence. He was unpopular with both Jews and Romans.

The commander sat on a dais near the priests, studying the Sadducees and Pharisees, who were whispering among themselves, for they had been caught unawares by the order for the trial. Nobody knew what the charges were and there was a good deal of speculation about them.

It was Paul, tired of waiting, who started the proceedings off.

'My brethren,' he said loudly and clearly to the Pharisees. 'Listen and I will tell you what you want to know. All my life I have lived before God with a clear conscience . . .'

Immediately Ananias interrupted in fury, 'Strike him on the mouth!'

A guard stepped forward and struck Paul across the face. He swung round and pointing at the high priest cried, 'God will strike you, you whitewashed wall! Do you sit there pretending to judge me by the Law, yet against the Law order me to be struck?'

There was a murmur in the court, and a temple guard threatened him with upraised hand, asking if he dared to insult God's high priest.

'Brethren' said Paul, calmer now, 'I had forgotten that he

was the high priest.'

Ananias silenced him. Hurriedly, he declared that he found Paul guilty of blasphemy, treason and sorcery. Gamaliel rose swiftly to protest, saying that he could not be found guilty, as he had had no chance to speak in his own defence.

'He has no defence,' declared Ananias with finality. 'I have heard witnesses who have sworn to his guilt. I beg you to control yourself, Rabbi Gamaliel. Remember the commander's presence. He has asked me to see justice done according to our Law. Do not let us be divided.'

He signalled to the guards to seize the prisoner, but Paul appealed to the Pharisees, crying out that he was one of them, and like them lived in hope of a life after death. It was for this belief that he was being tried.

Some of the Pharisees leapt to their feet. This was the strongest bone of contention between them and the Sadducees.

Gamaliel spoke for them all. 'We find no fault in this man. Who knows, perhaps a spirit or an angel has spoken to him as he claims. We will not doubt the word of a brother. Let your witnesses prove him to be a liar.'

With a nervous eye on the commander, Ananias called for silence in the court. 'We demand the death penalty for Saul of Tarsus,' he said, but the Pharisees demanded loudly that Paul be allowed to speak. The commander had had enough; he called for order in the court, and when there was silence he announced that since the court seemed undecided about the charges against Paul, he would keep him in protective custody for a few days. Meanwhile he hoped the high priest would see to it that the temple courts were not used for violent demonstrations on matters concerning Jewish religion and law.

With that he stepped down from the dais, and signing to Paul to follow him, left the court.

In a cell in the barracks Paul sat in deep dejection. He was distressed at what had happened in court, and worried too over Luke, who had got away unmolested by the crowd, but would be anxiously waiting for news. He had thought it wise not to try to get in touch with him, for fear of directing attention to him and so endangering him also.

His sad thoughts were interrupted by the opening of his cell door. His guard, with whom he was on good terms, came in with a young man.

'There's someone to see you.'

Paul rose and looked at the boy in surprise. The soldier, reminding the visitor that he could not stay long, left them alone together, with the door open.

'Who are you?' asked Paul.

'Saul of Tarsus.'

'*Saul of Tarsus?*' repeated Paul in amazement.

'Yes, I'm your nephew.'

'My sister's son?'

Saul nodded. Paul embraced his nephew, overcome with emotion. When he could speak, he told the boy that his sister had only been a child when he left Tarsus. And now, he learnt from Saul, her son was seventeen, and the family had come to live in Jerusalem, where Saul was studying with Rabbi Gamaliel.

The boy kept looking nervously at the open door, with the guard outside waiting. He spoke urgently. 'Listen, I came to warn you. They're plotting to kill you.'

'Who are?' asked Paul.

'Some of the Sadducees. They've taken a vow; they've even told the high priest about it.'

Paul pointed out that they could hardly reach him in prison—in a fortress guarded by the Roman army, but the boy went on in an anxious undertone.

'Yes, I know, that's where the plot comes in. The high priest has agreed to ask the commander to have you brought down to stand trial again ... something about fresh evidence ... Anyway, these men plan to be in wait outside the court and assassinate you as you are taken down.'

Paul was silent for a moment. Then he said how brave Saul had been to risk his life by coming. If they found out what he had done... The boy interrupted to ask what his uncle would do.

'We must warn the commander,' said Paul, 'so that he is prepared. Will you go to him and tell him what you have told me? I think he'll see you. He is a just man.'

They were interrupted by the soldier, who came back to say that the visitor must go now, as his time was up.

'Officer,' said Paul, 'please take this young man to see the commander. He has something of great importance to tell him—something that concerns the safety of a Roman citizen.'

The soldier was rather taken aback by the request, and said at first that he couldn't do it, but then he relented, and promised to see what he could do. He stood, waiting to lock the door, while Saul turned for a last word with his uncle.

'Mother sent this money,' he said, handing over a leather bag he carried at his belt. 'It's part of what grandfather left. She says you should have it.'

'God bless you, son,' said Paul. His dejection had gone at the threat of new danger, and he was happy at finding his nephew—and a nephew who had taken such risks for him. Even the sound of the door being locked on him once more did not worry him now. 'Perhaps this is not the end,' he thought. 'Perhaps after all I shall get to Rome.'

It was still early morning when the soldier knocked on the commander's door, and was told to go in. Saul felt very scared now, but he went in and stood erect before the commander, while the soldier explained that he was a relative of the prisoner with something urgent to say.

The commander was interested, and ready to hear anything that might throw light on the mystery of his prisoner. He saw, however, that the boy was nervous of speaking in front of the soldier, so he led him to the far side of the room, out of earshot, and told him to speak.

With nervous haste, Saul poured out the story of the plot to kill his uncle. 'If he leaves these barracks he'll not reach the court room alive, sir. At the meeting last night more than forty Jews bound themselves under a curse that they would neither eat nor drink until they'd killed him. They're posted all round outside, sir.'

'What has your uncle done,' asked Claudius Lysias, 'to turn priests into assassins?' and when the boy said defensively that his uncle had done nothing against the Law, the commander sighed. He was no nearer the heart of the mystery, but at least now there was a reason to take action and refer the matter to higher authority.

He told Saul to go home, and to be careful to speak to nobody about the matter. Then he dismissed him, and the boy went out into the morning sunshine, while in his room the commander gave orders for a party of seventy horsemen and 200 armed troops to be standing by at nine o'clock that night, with a horse for the prisoner Paul of Tarsus, ready to take him to Cæsarea.

Then Claudius Lysias took pen and ink and began to write a letter.

That night Paul was taken from his cell and down the steps of the barracks. There in the dusk he saw a great gathering of armed men and horses. He was mounted on a horse, and the cavalcade moved off, with him in their midst.

They were watched by a solitary figure: Luke, who could not rest till he knew what was to happen to Paul. All day he had kept watch, unseen, outside the fortress which housed the barracks. When he saw the cavalcade move off he found a horse and rode hard so he could catch up with the armed men and follow them to Cæsarea.

In Cæsarea Paul was kept under guard, while a messenger took Claudius Lysias's letter to the governor's house. Felix was an elderly man and care-worn, but a good governor. He ordered his clerk to read the letter, and learnt that he was to try a prisoner sent from Jerusalem.

'This man,' read out the clerk, 'was seized by the Jews and was on the point of being murdered by them when I arrived with my troops and rescued him, having learned that he was a Roman citizen. I discovered that he was being accused over some question or questions of their Law, but that there was no charge against him which deserved either death or imprisonment. Now, however, I have received private information of a plot against his life so I have sent him to you without delay. I will notify his accusers that if they wish to press their charges they must go to Cæsarea and do so in your presence.'

The governor asked where this man was, and when he was told that the prisoner was under guard at Herod's palace, said briskly, 'Well, see that he's decently treated. He's a Roman citizen. What sort of a man is he? Rich?'

'He's very shabbily dressed, sir,' the centurion who had brought the letter told him, 'but he seems to have plenty of money with him.'

'Friends?' asked the governor.

'There's a Greek with him, sir, a doctor, name of Luke.'

'Well, let him have free access to the prisoner. What's his name?'

'The Jews call him Saul, sir, but I think he likes to be known as Paul.'

The governor smiled, and commented that he was obviously proud of his Roman citizenship. He asked where Paul was from, and learnt that he was from Tarsus, his own province.

'I'll hear the case when his accusers arrive from Jerusalem,' he said.

Five days later Paul was brought to the court room to appear before the Governor Felix. The high priest, Ananias, had come down from Jerusalem bringing with him a skilful lawyer, Tertullus, to state the case of the prosecution.

Paul sat in chains, comforted to know that Luke was near him in the court as Tertullus rose to open the proceedings.

'Your excellency,' said Tertullus smoothly, 'it is owing to your just government that we enjoy unbroken peace, and owing to your wise care that the state of this nation has been improved in every way. All this we acknowledge with the deepest gratitude. I have no wish to weary your excellency with a long discourse, but I beg you to give me a brief hearing with your customary courtesy.

'The simple fact is that we have found this man, Saul or Paul

of Tarsus, to be an absolute pest, stirring up sedition and endangering the peace among Jews all over the world. He is the
ringleader of a sect called "The Nazarenes", and was actually
violating the temple when we arrested him. We would have
tried him according to our own Law, but the Commander
Claudius took him out of our hands, with great violence, and
insisted that the case must be tried before your excellency. For
our part we regret that your excellency should be troubled with
this matter, but if you wish to interrogate the prisoner, you will
discover for yourself the truth of the accusations against him.'

Tertullus sat down, and there was a murmur of approval
from the priests. The governor consulted his clerk, and read
over the notes he had made. In a low voice Felix asked what the
prosecution meant by 'Nazarenes', and was told they were
followers of a Jew called Jesus of Nazareth crucified some years
before.

'Oh, that fellow, yes,' said the governor. 'I've heard about
him.' And then in a louder voice he said, 'Call the prisoner.'

The clerk did so, and Paul rose, his eyes briefly meeting
Luke's before he turned towards the governor and spoke. He
said that he had no fears in putting his case, since the governor
was well acquainted with Jewish law. Twelve days earlier he had
gone up to Jerusalem for the Feast of Pentecost. He had never
disputed with anyone in the temple, nor had he gathered a
crowd either in the synagogues or anywhere in the city, nor
could the prosecution show proof of any of the charges they
had brought against him.

'What about this sect, the Nazarenes?' asked the governor.

'They call it a sect. We call it a Way,' Paul answered. 'The way
of worshipping the God of our fathers by faith in his Messiah.
They call this heresy. It is not heresy, for I put my trust in all
that is written in the Law and the prophets. I share with them
the hope in the life to come. With this hope before me I do my
utmost to live my life with a clear conscience before God and
man.'

The governor told him to give the court an account of what
happened in Jerusalem; and Paul explained to him that after

some years' absence he had come there to bring money that had been collected for the poor of his nation, and to attend certain ceremonies in the temple. At these ceremonies, needless to say, his friend Luke, a Gentile had remained outside in the courtyard. It was when Paul came out to join him that the trouble had started. Some Jews from Asia had incited the crowd to attack him.

'These are the men who should be standing before you today,' said Paul. 'I notice they are not here. But the high priest is here; therefore he should be called upon to tell you whether they could find me guilty of any crime when I stood before the council of the Sanhedrin.'

There was silence in court for a moment, until Felix asked if the lord high priest had anything to add to this evidence. Tertullus looked at Ananias for instructions, but Ananias shook his head.

'Nothing to add to the charges already made, your excellency,' said Tertullus, to which Felix replied that he could not find the prisoner guilty on the evidence available. Commander Lysias would be instructed to make further inquiries in Jerusalem. Meanwhile Paul would be kept in custody, on remand, but his friends could visit him and he would have a reasonable amount of liberty.

He rose and dismissed the court.

For two years no further evidence came from Jerusalem either for Paul or against him. Meanwhile a new high priest had been appointed in Jerusalem, and a new governor, Festus, in Cæsarea.

Festus, a younger man than his predecessor, was entertaining the young King Herod Agrippa II. The last and probably the best of his line, he was still on good terms with Rome, and had the appearance and bearing of a young Roman. With him was his sister, Berenice—a gay and witty young woman, who had been married twice, but now lived with her brother to whom she was devoted. Although she was a very worldly woman she went in for sudden extremes of religious fervour.

In Festus's room the two young people were drinking wine with him, and Agrippa asked the governor how he enjoyed his new office.

'Tolerably well,' was Festus's reply.

They spoke of Jerusalem, and of Claudius Lysias, whom Festus thought a good man.

'I got rid of the high priest, Ananias,' said Agrippa. 'The new one I've appointed, Ismael, has more idea of justice, I think.'

'It may be so,' said Festus, doubtfully. 'I didn't know the last one. I confess that when it comes to the intricacies of Jewish law and custom, I find myself bewildered.'

Agrippa laughed. You had to be trained to it from babyhood, he said, as he had had to be—though in many ways, he added, he felt more Roman than Jew.

'I've an unsolved mystery on my hands at the moment,' said Festus, 'which I suppose could be called a matter of religion.' And he told his guests about Paul, a Jew who had now been in custody for two years. He had been offered the chance to go back to Jerusalem to be tried again there, but had now appealed to Cæsar.

'Then he must go to Cæsar,' said Agrippa, while Berenice, intrigued, begged to know what Paul had done.

Festus said that it was difficult for him to make head or tail of the case now, but it was all to do with Jewish religious beliefs. Paul had been accused of being Christian. 'Do you know what that means?' Festus asked, and when Agrippa said no, he explained: 'Well, as far as I can make out it's something to do with a man named Jesus who died, and whom Paul claims is still alive.'

Berenice leant forward eagerly. *Jesus?* I know that name.'

'A very common name, my dear,' said Agrippa.

'No ... Don't you remember, Agrippa, when we were children,' said Berenice. 'During the famine when we were with father in Jerusalem? ... I've never forgotten it. Those men outside the palace who were feeding the people and healing the sick kept on saying "Jesus" ... "Of Nazareth", wasn't it?'

'I'd no idea there were any members of the "Jesus" sect still in the country,' said Agrippa. 'Why, it's been going on for years. And it's very strange, you know, that I should come across it. My family has had clashes with Jesus for three generations. I'll be the fourth! My great-grandfather, Herod the Great, you know, was king of Judea when he got the idea that a child born in Bethlehem was going to become "King of the Jews" and he ordered all the male children in the district to be slaughtered.'

'But the baby Jesus escaped,' said Berenice. 'Just like Moses in the bulrushes. I suppose his parents hid him.'

The next Herod to hear of Jesus was their uncle Antipas, about thirty years later. A man had been going around Judea preaching that Jesus was the Messiah. Antipas took this to mean he was a rival king of the Jews, and had the man beheaded. And afterwards Antipas had sat in judgement on Jesus himself.

'Indeed?' said Festus. 'So Jesus *was* a trouble-maker?'

'Well, so they said,' Agrippa agreed. 'I've often wondered about it myself, knowing how the high priests like to fabricate charges. Well, you've come across it already yourself. Anyway, he was accused by the Sanhedrin in the same way as this fellow Paul, and presented to the governor to be tried.'

'Pontius Pilate?'

'Yes, I think that was the name. Like you, he found it difficult to understand the charges made by the priests, so he sent Jesus to my uncle to see if he could help. My uncle got the impression that he was just a harmless lunatic.'

''But what's so fascinating,' said Berenice, her voice rising in excitement, 'is that this prisoner of yours should say that Jesus is still alive. That's why I think there is something magic about him.'

'Is Jesus dead then? Even though your uncle thought him harmless?' asked Festus.

'Oh yes,' said Agrippa. 'My uncle sent him back to Pilate who had him crucified.'

'But why should people *still* be talking about him and risk getting arrested for it too,' insisted Berenice. 'I think it's all very exciting. *Do* let's hear this man and try and find out some more.'

10
To Rome

PAUL had appealed to Cæsar and awaited the order to go to Rome. The two years of his imprisonment at Cæsarea were not wasted years, for although his hands were chained, with Luke's help he wrote many letters to strengthen and encourage the different churches.

He stood at the window of his cell one day, dictating one such letter, saying that although he was far away, in spirit he was by their side, watching like a proud father the steadfastness of their faith. As he spoke he lifted his water-jar and watered a little plant growing on the ledge. 'You are planted in Christ,' he said, 'and you will grow, as a plant grows out of the soil, drawing strength through the roots to stretch upwards and out-wards in joy and thankfulness to God . . .'

The door of the cell opened and Julius, the centurion, came in, with orders from the governor Festus that Paul was to be brought to the court room.

'Luke,' said Paul, 'perhaps the orders have come for me to go to Rome!'

Julius said that he had heard nothing about that but that Herod Agrippa was with the governor. 'He's a Jew like you,' he added, 'so maybe he's going to put in a word for you.'

Paul assured him that he was anxious to go to Rome—though, he added with a smile, it would be better to go without the chains.

This time the atmosphere of the court room was relaxed and easy, for it was more of a show to please the royal visitors than trial by law.

Paul took his place facing the governor, and the hush of curiosity at his entrance was followed by chatter, which ended when Festus rose to his feet, to explain that here was a man against whom the whole Jewish nation seemed to have taken up arms. He himself could not find any fault in him, certainly nothing to deserve death; but the prisoner had elected to go to Rome and present his case to the emperor.

'Now, I find myself in something of a dilemma,' he said, 'for since there is no specific charge against him, what can I say about him in my letter to his majesty?'

His audience laughed, and the governor went on to say that he fervently hoped King Agrippa would help to unravel the mystery of Paul of Tarsus.

Paul, called upon by the king to speak, appealed to him as a fellow Jew familiar with the customs and controversies of their race.

From his youth, he said, he had belonged to the strictest party of their religion, the Pharisees—a fact well known to all the Jews who had testified against him. 'I stand here in chains for one reason only—that I believe with my whole heart in the promise made to our fathers: the resurrection of the dead.'

Festus turned to look at Berenice, who gave a little smile of triumph and whispered to Agrippa, 'I told you so.'

'Tell us then,' said Agrippa, 'what quarrel the Jews in Jerusalem had with you and your beliefs.'

'I will tell you,' said Paul. 'The men that accused me pretend that they believe in the coming of the Messiah and in the resurrection. But when these two things in which they pretend to believe are put before them as living facts they cannot bear the truth. They will lie and cheat and persecute in the name of righteousness rather than accept the fulfilment of God's promises. For God's promise *has* been fulfilled. The Messiah has come to us in the person of Jesus of Nazareth whom God has raised from the dead.'

There was a murmur of incredulous laughter in the court. Agrippa was embarrassed, Festus bewildered. Only Berenice showed extreme excitement.

'Why,' asked Paul, 'does it seem incredible to you that God should raise the dead?'

Festus said that they were not disparaging his religious beliefs—only the application of them. They knew that Jesus of Nazareth had been crucified to death nearly thirty years earlier. How then could Paul say that God had raised him from the dead?'

'Because I have seen him,' said Paul calmly. Berenice could restrain herself no longer. 'When, where?' she asked.

'Two years after he was crucified,' Paul told her. 'I was not one of his disciples, you know, far from it. In those days it was I who was the persecutor, I who threw men into prison for daring to use the words "Jesus the Messiah", I who with the authority of the chief priests set out to distant cities to arrest any who believed in him. I had more hatred in my heart in those days for Jesus of Nazareth than the men who want to kill me today.'

'But tell us what you saw,' urged Agrippa.

Paul addressed himself directly to him. 'I saw the Messiah. He stood before me in a blaze of light more dazzling than the midday sun. It was Jesus.'

Agrippa leaned forward. 'How do you know?'

'He told me so,' replied Paul. 'Do you suppose that I, the greatest enemy of Jesus, would have invented such a story, and could have undertaken to preach even to Gentiles about Israel's Messiah if I had not seen him and received from him my commission?'

'What commission?'

'I'll tell you in his own words, King Agrippa. "I send you to open the eyes of the Gentiles, to turn them from darkness to light, from the power of Satan to God himself, so that through faith in me they will have their sins forgiven and receive their place among God's chosen people." Can you doubt that this was a heavenly vision? I had no doubt. I set myself to obey my Lord's command. That is why the Jews seized me in the temple, although what I preach is only what the prophets and Moses foretold: that the Christ should suffer and that he should rise from the dead.'

Agrippa had been unwillingly moved by Paul's sincerity, but Festus had become more and more bemused. Impatiently he burst out: 'You are raving, Paul. All your study and learning has made you mad!'

'No, I am not mad, your excellency,' said Paul. 'These things were prophesied and have come true. The king knows what I speak of. Tell me, King Agrippa, do you believe in the prophets?' The king didn't answer. He was embarrassed at being questioned Jew to Jew in this way. Undaunted, Paul continued: 'You do. I know you do.'

Agrippa gave an uneasy laugh. 'In another moment you'll be telling me I've become a Christian!'

Paul's voice rang out with all the fervour of his preaching days. 'I would to God that you and all who hear me today might stand where I stand.' He raised his fettered hands. 'Even with these chains.'

The governor and his royal guests talked together in undertones.

'You can't punish this man,' whispered Berenice. 'There's something holy about him.'

'He's certainly not a law-breaker,' commented Agrippa. 'But you say he has appealed to Cæsar?'

Festus nodded.

'Then to Cæsar he must go.'

So, a prisoner in chains, Paul began his journey to Rome. With other prisoners he was put on board a small coastal boat which sailed under the lee of Cyprus to the Asiatic seaport of Myra in Lycia, where Julius, the centurion in charge of them, bargained with the captain owner of an Alexandrian grain ship to take them to Italy.

The ship was already heavily loaded with grain and had a large crew. The captain was doubtful.

'It's a government order. You'll be well paid for it,' Julius reminded him.

'What about your prisoners, are they safe? I don't want any trouble on board, and I can't afford any delay.'

'You can see they're chained and well guarded,' said Julius.

The captain looked at the wretched, half-naked prisoners chained together by wrists and ankles. Then he noticed Paul standing a little apart from them with Luke.

'He's a special case, a Roman citizen,' said Julius. 'The governor's given orders he's to be treated as a passenger, not a prisoner. The other man's his friend, a doctor. He's had permission to travel with him.' The captain, glad to have a doctor on board, was prepared to make the best of this extra cargo of prisoners. And so they boarded the ship and set sail on the next stage of the journey to Rome.

They made slow progress because the wind was against them. Strong winds buffeted the huge central sail, while the men at the steering oars fought to keep the ship on course in the heavy seas. The wind grew to gale force, but at last after many days they reached the island of Crete, and coasting along the rocky south shore with great difficulty they took refuge in the little natural harbour called Fair Havens and lowered the sail and dropped anchor there.

As a favoured prisoner, though still in chains, Paul was in the cabin with the captain and Julius when they held a consultation. The captain, anxious at the delay, was not in a good temper.

'The weather's always chancy at this time of year,' he said, 'but I've never had to drop anchor here before.'

'I suppose we'll stay here until the weather improves?' asked Julius.

'It won't improve until the spring now. We've taken two months to get this far. It's the extra weight on board that's slowed us down. I've got my cargo to deliver, sir, and I can't afford to spend all winter here.'

'I'm thinking of the safety of the ship and those on board.'

'The safety of the ship is my responsibility.'

Suddenly Paul spoke up: 'Then you must see that it would be madness to up-anchor in this weather. Better delay than lose the ship, crew, cargo and all.'

'I think we must leave the decision to the captain,' said Julius quickly.

'I do not intend to put out to sea in this storm,' said the captain. 'But if the wind changes and we get one from the southeast, we could coast along to Phoenix at the western tip of the island. It's a good-sized town with a real harbour. We might find a ship to take some of my cargo or your prisoners. 'It's the extra weight that's done for us as much as the weather.'

The next day as Luke sat writing his diary and the captain and Julius, their argument forgotten, played at dice, Paul sat listening to the roar of the gale. It seemed to him to be growing less. Suddenly feet were heard pounding along the deck and the helmsman rushed in with great excitement.

'Wind's changed, sir!' he shouted.

The captain threw down the dice and hurried out on to the deck with the helmsman, and soon the ship was alive with shouts and running feet. 'All hands on deck . . . Stand by to weigh anchor . . . Stand by to hoist sail.'

After the days of enforced idleness the men sprang to their work with a will, and a cheer went up as the huge sail billowed out in the south-east breeze and the ship sailed out of Fair Havens. The helmsman followed the plan suggested by the captain and kept the ship close in to the high red cliffs. There were dangerous currents only a little way out at sea, and the only safe course was hugging the shore.

All seemed to be going well, when suddenly the wind changed yet again and a terrific gale, a north-easter, swept down on them from the mountains, driving them away from the shore. The helmsman clung to his steering oar, desperately trying to hold course. The deck sloped dangerously, the port side nearly under water. Paul and Luke battled their way along the deck to lend a hand to the sailors who were using all their strength to keep the sail from taking the full blast of the gale. The red cliffs that were to shelter them looked ominous now, and as the ship rose and fell in the turbulent sea it seemed as though they must be dashed on to the rocks. The captain saw the danger and decided to risk the open sea. 'Let her run before the wind.'

The helmsman let the steering oars go. The men on the sail ropes eased their grip and the ropes were torn from their hands. Some of them were thrown on the deck by the spin of the ship as she heeled round and took the full blast of the gale in her sails. The roar of the wind and the pounding seas were deafening, and the ship's timbers creaked and groaned as though she would be torn apart. Below in the hold the prisoners screamed and cried out in terror as they were rolled about helpless in their chains. Paul went down to try to comfort them.

On deck the captain shouted another order 'Get the long-boat aboard.'

The helmsman looked over the stern into the raging sea where the longboat which they towed behind them was completely submerged.

'Can't haul her in in this, sir.'

'Get her aboard,' repeated the captain. 'We may need her.' He took the steering oar while the helmsman ordered a party of sailors to the rope securing the longboat 'Heave! Heave! Heave!' he shouted. The boat rose above the surface and was drawn to the side of the ship, but just as it seemed that they had a fast hold, one of the men lost his grip, and the rope began to slip through their hands.

'All hands! All hands!' cried the helmsman. Luke left an in-jured sailor he was tending, and Paul hurried up from among the prisoners, and soon the longboat was aboard. But the helmsman told the captain of a new anxiety.

'The ship'll break apart if this goes on, sir,' he said.

The captain nodded. 'Think we can undergirt her?' he asked.

'Not a hope, sir,' said the helmsman. 'Not while she's travelling at this speed.'

'If we could steer to the lee of one of the islands there might be enough shelter. Have a man ready and send someone aloft to keep a lookout.'

'Aloft, sir?' queried the helmsman in amazement.

'That's what I said,' answered the captain.

A few moments later a sailor, stripped to the waist and drenched by spray, was climbing up the mast, his body flattened against it from time to time by the force of the wind. He hauled himself up to the cross-bar, and sat there precariously. The captain stood by to give the order to change course.

Suddenly there was a shout from the look-out. 'Land . . . land ahoy!'

'It'll be the island of Clauda, I reckon, sir,' said the helmsman, and when the captain ordered him to steer a course towards it, he protested that they would be driven on to the rocks.

'That would be better than breaking up in the open seas,' said the captain.

The helmsman kept the land on their starboard side and steered to the west, till they were in the lee of the island of Clauda. There they dropped anchor and lowered the sail, and there Paul and Luke watched the sailors cast a rope into the water at the bows and drag it towards midship. They did the same aft. This was 'undergirting'— running cables under the hull to take the strain off the timbers. It was usually only done in harbour. The men cheered as the ropes were finally secured.

The captain had now done all that he could to save the ship and the lives of the men on board. Night fell, and with it there came yet another storm. The slight protection of the island and the sea anchor that had been put out were useless against the driving elements, and once again they began to drift. To steer was impossible. For fourteen nights they were at the mercy of the storm. There was no sun to cheer them by day, no stars to guide them by night. All hope of being save seemed lost.

On the morning of the fifteenth day the storm still raged. Paul lay sleeping in the cabin. The captain and Julius sat silent and dejected. The captain looked up as Luke came in and asked how his crew was—for Luke had been giving what help he could to both crew and prisoners.

'In a bad way for the most part, sir,' said Luke. 'They've not eaten for days.'

'Why not?' asked the captain. 'We've still enough food. We didn't throw that overboard with my cargo.'

Luke explained that much of it had been spoiled by sea water, and most of the men were too sick or too scared to eat. The captain was concerned and said that he must go to them, for once the men lost heart the ship was really lost. But he had nothing of comfort to say to them.

There was a sudden movement from the corner where Paul had been sleeping. He rose to his feet. 'Tell them to take heart,' he said. 'Not one of them will die.'

The other three looked at him in amazement, and the captain asked how they could say that, when they knew it not to be true.

'It is true,' said Paul calmly. 'While I was sleeping the Lord God spoke to me in a dream. He has promised that even though we lose the ship not one life will be lost.'

The captain, who was a superstitious man, and ready now to grab at any straw, asked what God he was talking about, to which Paul replied, 'The one God.'

There was a rush of air, and the gale howled more loudly in the tiny cabin as a soldier burst in and forced the door shut again against the wind. He spoke urgently in an undertone to Julius, who explained to the others that some of the crew were lowering the longboat as if they meant to abandon the ship.

'Unless they stay aboard no one can be saved,' said Paul.

Taking command of the situation, Julius told the soldier they must cut the rope, and drawing their swords they rushed on deck.

There was some protest from the men, who pretended they were putting out sea anchors. But Julius looked over the side and saw the boat in the water. In an instant he slashed with his sword at the rope and the longboat slid away from the ship, was seized by the huge waves, tossed high—and disappeared from sight.

An outcry rose from the sailors, who felt their last hope was gone. They turned in fury on Julius, but more soldiers with drawn swords came to his side. Still the sailors menaced them, yelling threats against the howling wind—they had little to lose, and fear of hunger and the waves was greater than their fear of swords at this moment.

Suddenly, above the clamour, a voice called, 'Come and eat!'

Soldiers and mutinous sailors turned at the sound of it, and saw Paul standing with a basket of bread in his arms. Reluctantly at first, the sailors gathered round him, then slowly squatted on their haunches to take the hunks of bread he handed them. Luke helped a sick sailor towards the others, and some who lay about the deck, ill with hunger, found strength enough to crawl towards Paul for their share. Paul handed the basket to Luke, who passed it round; but the men were too amazed to eat. They stared at Paul, wondering, for the bread was good and not sodden with sea-water.

Paul took a piece of the bread, and then almost to himself said the familiar blessing: 'Thank, you Lord God, king of the universe, who brings forth bread from the earth.'

Paul ate, and the men followed suit, some ravenously, the sick ones with an effort. The captain and Julius looked at each other questioningly, and there was a flicker of hope on the captain's face. As they stood there in the sudden silence, the only sounds the monotonous whine of the wind and the creaking of the boat, the helmsman, who had gone to the bows, a piece of bread in his hand, came back to speak in an urgent whisper to the captain, who followed him to the bows. He pointed ahead.

'I don't know what land it is, sir,' said the helmsman. 'But whatever it is, there is a chance of beaching the ship if there is a sandy beach.'

The captain was staring hard at the coastline, and said with rising excitement: 'There's a bay right ahead. Looks like sand.' He made his decision. 'We'll risk it, cut the anchor ropes, hoist the foresail and let her go with the wind.'

By now the rest of the crew had seen the coast, and echoed the helmsman's jubilant shout of 'Land ahoy!' Then, with fresh hope, they leapt to obey his orders. In a moment they had cut the anchor ropes, and were standing by for further commands.

A sailor ran in from the stern. 'What about the steering-oars, sir?' he asked. 'They'll likely swing out and take us off course.'

'Cut them adrift,' ordered the helmsman.

Julius had joined the captain in the bows, where four sailors were waiting by the reefed foresail. The captain was studying the direction of the wind before giving the order to hoist sail. The helmsman came forward to report that they were free of the anchors and steering oars.

'Good,' said the captain. 'The wind's right for us now, and the bay's straight ahead. Hoist sail!'

The four sailors hauled on the ropes. The foresail leapt upwards and billowed out into the wind, and the crew cheered as the ship sailed on a straight course for the island.

It was Julius who gave the first alarm of danger, pointing to a dark line on the coast, visible when the waves lifted them high. The helmsman scrambled on to the prow, and gave a cry of horror. 'It's rocks,' he shouted.

'Haul in the foresail!' ordered the captain, and the crew struggled to obey, but they were powerless against the driving wind. The foresail stayed up, and the ship ran forward without check, straight on to a partly submerged reef. There was a sudden grinding jolt and the noise of splintering wood. They were all thrown to the deck, as the prow seemed to rise into the air and lurch over to one side. Heavy seas began to break over the stern, and a moment later a huge wave smashed against the mast and brought it down. It toppled slowly sideways and fell into the sea.

From the hold a frenzied group of manacled prisoners struggled on to the deck, and were stopped there by a soldier with drawn sword, who appealed to Julius to give the order to kill the prisoners. 'They've broken loose, and they'll try and swim for it, sir,' he said.

'No,' said Julius. 'Release them and let any who can swim jump overboard and save themselves if they can.'

Only the bows of the ship were now above water, and the captain saw that there was not a moment to lose. 'Every man for himself!' he ordered, and at once the prisoners, the crew and the soldiers began to leap or dive overboard.

Julius removed the chains from Paul's hands, and told him to save himself, but instead of jumping into the sea Paul turned to a cowering group of prisoners, too terrified to move. He told them to save themselves, and they said it was useless—they could not swim.

'Nor can I,' said Paul cheerfully. 'We'll go together. We'll find a bit of wreckage to cling to. Come on, have courage, brothers.' He dragged the nearest man to his feet. 'Come on, all of you, whether you can swim or not. There's plenty of wood afloat that'll support you.'

With Luke now to help him, Paul guided and persuaded the prisoners into the water, pushing them towards drifting pieces of wreckage, and supporting one whose weakness made it impossible for him to cling unaided. The waves carried them nearer and nearer to the beach, and Paul's voice could be heard above the thunder of the waves, urging them to hold on, for they would soon be safe.

And safe they were. Not a single life was lost. Bruised and exhausted, they reached the beach. Most of them were too spent to do more than lie on the wet sand. They were cold, and their wet clothes clung to them, heavy with sea-water and sand.

Almost at once the natives of the island, who had watched the ship foundering on the rocks, were there to help them. They spoke a strange language, but they treated the shipwrecked strangers with uncommon kindness, and lit fires on the beach so that they could warm and dry themselves. Luke wandered among them all, attending to injuries and reassuring those who needed comfort, while Paul carried more wood to the fire, and helped some of the most exhausted men towards its warmth.

One of the islanders suddenly pointed along the beach, and

called out, 'Publius . . . Publius.'

A figure in a Roman toga was coming towards them. He was the chief official, and Julius went to meet him, giving him a Roman handshake. He was relieved to find that the man could speak his language, and he quickly explained their position to him.

'We shall have to stay on your island, sir,' he said, 'until we can pick up another ship sailing for Italy. What is the name of the island?'

'Malta,' said Publius, and suddenly gave a cry of horror and pointed at Paul, who had thrown more wood on the fire, and now stood with a small snake wound round his wrist. 'The snake!' cried Publius.

The other natives began to talk excitedly, and Paul winced suddenly with the sharp, sudden pain as the snake bit him. Then he tore the snake from his wrist, threw it into the flames, and unconcernedly went on feeding wood to the fire.

Luke strode quickly to him, asking urgently to see his wrist, for the snake bite was deadly, but when he looked . . . there was no mark.

Paul smiled at his bewilderment. 'I haven't survived storm and shipwreck,' he said, 'to be killed by a snake. Don't forget we are to go to Rome.'

Excited chatter broke out among the islanders as word spread that this man had been bitten by a deadly viper and yet was unhurt. Some of them came and knelt round Paul, touching his clothes and murmuring reverently in their strange language.

'What are they saying?' Julius asked Publius.

'They think your friend must be a god,' answered Publius. 'Who is he?'

Julius told him that he was a prisoner from Jerusalem, going to Rome to be tried before Cæsar. 'It's my belief,' Julius added, 'we'd not have survived but for him.'

'Sir,' said Publius, 'you will stay at my house, and I beg you to bring this man with you so that I and my family may get to know him. The rest of your party will be given shelter in our villages until we can find a ship to take you to Italy.'

They stayed on the shore long enough to see that all the men—soldiers, sailors and prisoners—were made welcome by the kindly natives; then they made their way to the chief official's house, where his wife and servants hurried to provide fresh clothes and food for Julius, Paul, Luke and the captain. They were very thankful to have such hospitality, and to sleep safely on land that night.

Malta was their home for the next three months. During those three months Paul and Luke did a great deal of work among the islanders who were ill. It began when Paul laid his hands on Publius's old father, who had a high fever with dysentery. At Paul's touch the old man, who had been tossing about restlessly, suddenly became quiet.

That was the beginning, but news of it got around, and before long mothers brought sick babies to Paul, and the village square outside Publius's house was full of people, men, women and children, some lying on mattresses, some supported by friends. Luke, as a doctor, examined and tended them; and Paul laid his hands upon them.

At last Julius found a ship that had spent the winter in harbour and was due to sail for Italy.

When the day came for them to leave Malta, all the people came to the harbour to see them off, many of them weeping. The islanders loaded gifts upon them: baskets of fruit, embroidered linen, garlands of flowers, bundles of gifts of all kinds. It was a beautiful spring morning when their ship, *The Twin Brothers*, sailed over the blue Mediterranean sea to Italy.

Once more Paul was a prisoner, making for Rome. Once more he was manacled, and in the company of other prisoners.

They reached Puetoli in Italy and began the long march to Rome along the Appian Way. Paul, tramping along manacled to Julius at the head of the straggling procession of prisoners and soldiers, suddenly stopped. Julius was brought up sharply and turned with a reprimand on his lips. But the look on Paul's face silenced him. It was transfigured with joy and the tear-filled eyes gazed along the road ahead. Julius followed their gaze and saw a young man racing towards them. Paul held out his arms, and panting and laughing the young man threw himself into their embrace.

'Timothy, my son.'

'Master!'

It was a moving reunion which Julius, chained as he was to Paul, shared with some embarrassment. About a hundred yards up the road stood the Three Taverns, a resting place for travellers on the Appian Way. He told Paul that they would be stopping there for a rest and that he could talk to his friend then. They continued the march, Timothy with his arm round Paul's shoulders. There at the Three Taverns was another surprise for Paul, for waiting by the roadside, their donkey beside them, stood Priscilla and Aquilla. The faithful old couple had made the long journey from Rome to greet their friend. Julius unfastened the chain from his own wrist, but left Paul's wrists chained together. He told Paul he could stay and talk with his friends for a few minutes and left them alone together while he went into the inn to refresh himself.

Paul sat on the side of the well with his old friends while Timothy washed his master's feet and Luke went to fetch food and wine for them.

'Why, it's like coming home,' said Paul. 'How did you know that I was going to Rome?'

'You wrote from Cæsarea that you were coming,' Priscilla explained. 'The brothers in Ephesus sent us word.'

'We're still at our old trade, tent-making,' Aquilla told him. 'We've got a nice little business on the banks of the Tiber. Merchants bring us news from all over the world.'

'And you, Timothy?' asked Paul.

'I was in Philippi, you know,' said Timothy, 'with Lydia. She heard from some of the traders that you had appealed to Cæsar. I came here as fast as I could. I was afraid I might be too late.'

'You might have been if we hadn't been shipwrecked,' Paul told him. Timothy was eager to know what had happened, but

Paul was more anxious to hear how they, and the little church that met in their house, had fared than to waste time telling them about his own adventures.

Priscilla assured him that the church was faithful and strong, though not growing in numbers as they might wish.

'The Lord guided me to Rome,' said Paul. 'There is a purpose in that. Whether I am to die here or to live we don't know. But whichever way I go, one thing is certain. The church of Christ will live.'

After they had had their bread and wine Julius returned and said they must be on their way. He asked if Aquilla and Priscilla would be going with them, and when the old couple said yes, he reminded them that it was forty miles to the city.

'That's all right,' said Priscilla cheerfully. 'We've done the journey many times. We have our donkey. May our friend walk with us?'

'Very well,' said Julius. 'But he'll have to be chained again when we get within sight of the city. It's the law, you understand.'

Aquilla said they understood, and thanked Julius. They went to fetch the donkey, and Julius stared after them for a moment, then went off to reassemble his troops and prisoners.

It was a long and weary march to Rome, but much less wearisome for the five friends than for the soldiers and prisoners behind them, for there was much news to exchange, and many loving messages to be given from old friends and a great deal to tell about the progress of the churches.

When at last they came in sight of the great city of Rome, the cavalcade stopped at a camp just outside the walls. There a message was sent to the tent of Afranius Burrus, the captain of the Praetorian guard, telling him that the Centurion Julius had arrived from Cæsarea with a party of prisoners, one of special importance as he was due to appear before the emperor.

'Ah yes,' said Burrus, 'I've had a letter about him. From the Governor Festus in Cæsarea. Paul of Tarsus, eh?'

He sent for Julius, and when he was brought in told him curtly that he had been a long time getting there. Julius explained that he and his prisoners had been shipwrecked, and had to swim for their lives off the coast of Malta.

'Lose any prisoners?' inquired Burrus.

'No, sir. Not a single life was lost. Neither crew nor prisoner. Something of a miracle that.'

Burrus asked if the Jew, Paul of Tarsus, had given any trouble.

'Oh no, sir,' replied Julius. 'He travelled as a passenger. The governor's order, you know. We were all glad to have him on board, I can tell you.'

'Why?' asked the captain.

'He has a way with him,' was the answer. 'A kind of power. It seems as though he knows what is going to happen.' Julius went on to explain about the shipwreck, and how Paul had promised the men that not one of them would die.

Burrus was interested—and curious; but he said they would have to wait and see what the emperor made of Paul. Meanwhile he could hire lodgings for himself while he was waiting for his trial—though he would have to be guarded.

Paul sat in his lodgings in Rome, lightly chained to a Roman soldier who sat beside him, as Luke ushered in six elders from the synagogue. The Jews looked wary and suspicious, though not hostile, and Paul greeted them formally.

'I must thank you for coming here to visit me,' he said. 'As you see'—and he indicated his chain—' I am not able to attend the synagogue as I would wish. Please be seated.'

The six Jews sat on the floor, while Luke stayed by the door.

Paul explained to them why he, their fellow Jew, was in Rome as a prisoner. He assured them that he had done nothing against the customs of their ancestors. But in spite of this the Jews in Jerusalem had tried to have him put to death and had handed him over to the Roman authorities, bringing false charges against him. He was not in Rome to bring charges against the Jews, but to defend himself before Cæsar. 'Indeed,' he added, 'it is for the *hope* of Israel that I wear this chain.'

'The hope of Israel?' asked one of the Jews.

'You know what that hope is. The promised Messiah,' said Paul, at which the Jews began to murmur among themselves. Paul caught the words 'Christians' and 'trouble in Asia'. Then the spokesman addressed Paul.

'It is true that we have not received any letters about you from Jerusalem, nor has word reached us officially or un-officially. We shall be interested to hear what you have to say, although we do know that this sect who preach of a Messiah—Christians, I believe they are called—have not met with approval in the synagogues of other countries.'

'But do not let it be said of you in Rome, my brothers,' pleaded Paul, 'that you too rejected your Messiah. The greatest anguish of my heart, the pain that never leaves me, is this knowledge that so many of my fellow Israelites have failed to grasp the inheritance that is theirs. Indeed, I could almost wish myself cut off from the love of Christ, if by so doing I could bring my brothers to him.'

He went on to remind them what riches the Jews had been given. They were God's chosen people to whom he had revealed his glory, given the Law, taught the way of true worship, sent his prophets and now sent his Messiah. And yet it was his own people who shut their hearts against the word of God.

'The word of God?' demanded one of the Jews, shocked. 'You claim to bring the word of God?'

'How else should God speak to his children but through the mouths of his messengers?' asked Paul quietly. 'Do you suppose that God's last words to man were the ten commandments that he gave us through Moses? What about the Holy One the prophets spoke of? The saviour who was to draw people closer to God the Father?'

There were some uneasy murmurs among the Jews, but Paul continued.

'I tell you it is against *him* that the Jews close their hearts. Against the Christ whom God has sent so that we are no longer alone in our fight against sin and disease; so that we have at last a chance to build God's kingdom on earth with the help of his holy Son, Jesus the Christ.'

There were more murmurs from his listeners. Some of the Jews were interested and impressed, but others were sure that this was a dangerous doctrine.

Their spokesman rose. 'Rest assured, Paul,' he said, 'we have no quarrel with you on any point of Law, and we wish you well at your trial, but this doctrine of yours cannot be accepted by the synagogue . . .'

He was interrupted by the others, some saying they must hear more evidence before they could either reject or accept, others declaring angrily that they had heard enough, and that what Paul said was heresy. Still arguing, they took their leave of him, saying they would pray for him.

But as they began to file out Paul stopped them. 'They were true words,' he said, 'that the Holy Spirit put into the mouth of the prophet Isaiah: "You will hear and never understand. You will see but never perceive". . . . But be assured of this: the salvation our God has sent has been sent also to the Gentiles and they *will* listen to it.'

The Jews stood staring at him uneasily for a moment. Then without another word they left the room, and Paul, still chained to the soldier watched them go.

Two years went by, and still Paul waited in Rome for his trial. He had many visitors, both Jews and Gentiles, who came to hear from Paul's own lips the story of the Lord Jesus Christ. Even though he was a prisoner it was still Paul's shoulders that carried the burden of all the churches.

At Paul's dictation Luke wrote many letters to cheer and strengthen them. One of these letters was to his 'beloved son' Timothy.

> '. . . Take your share of suffering as a loyal soldier in Christ's army, and the Lord will give you understanding. Remember, always as the centre of everything Jesus Christ, the man born from the line of David and risen from the dead to be our saviour. . . . The time for my departure is near. I have fought the good fight, I have finished my course, I have kept the faith . . . Only Luke is with me now.'